Cassell
Wellington House
125 Strand
London WC2R 0BB

370 Lexington Avenue
New York
NY10017 - 6550

First published 1996
Reprinted 1997, 1998

British Library Cataloguing-in-Publication Data
A catalogue record for this book is available from the British Library.

ISBN 0–304–33338–7

Library of Congress Cataloging-in-Publication Data
Hek, Gill.
    Making sense of research: an introduction for nurses/Gill
Hek, Maggie Judd, Pam Moule.
        p.   cm.
    Includes bibliographical references and index.
    ISBN 0–304–33338–7
    1. Nursing—Research—Methodology.   I.   Judd, Maggie.   II. Moule,
Pam.   III. Title.
    [DNLM: 1. Nursing Research—methods.   WY 20.5
H473m 1996]
RT81.5.H45   1996
610.73'076–dc20
DNLM/DLC
for Library of Congress

95–26737
CIP

Typeset by Action Typesetting Limited, Gloucester
Printed and bound in Great Britain by
Redwood Books, Trowbridge, Wiltshire

MAKING SENSE OF RESEARCH

Also available from Cassell:

S. Chellen: *Information Technology for the Caring Professions*

S. Chellen: *Excel for Windows for the Caring Professions*

S. Chellen: *Word for Windows for the Caring Professions*

S. Chellen: *Wordperfect for the Caring Professions*

M. Herbert: *Planning a Research Project*

M. Jacobs: *The Care Guide*

C. Lashley: *Improving Study Skills*

R. Newell: *Developing Your Career in Nursing*

H. Schulze and W. Wirth: *Who Cares? Social Service Organizations and their Users*

MAKING SENSE OF RESEARCH
An Introduction for Nurses

Gill Hek
Maggie Judd
Pam Moule

CASSELL

CONTENTS

LIST OF TABLES

LIST OF FIGURES

FOREWORD

I am delighted to write the foreword for this book. It will fulfil a long-felt need of nurses and other health professionals who want to understand the principles of doing and using research within everyday practice.

Books about research are often criticized for being difficult to understand. This text takes challenging concepts and explains them very clearly, providing examples of practical application. In this way research principles become accessible and relevant to a wide readership.

The importance of developing critical skills is emphasized throughout, and the text will help the reader to gain this expertise. Each chapter is signposted with learning outcomes which are clearly developed in the text. Literature searches and reviews are skilfully explained. Key terms are defined and explained with practical examples.

The authors are to be congratulated on turning their experience in teaching and research into such a useful text. The book will obviously make a very valuable contribution to those practitioners who are responsive to the need to become research aware, and to base professional practice on sound evidence. Being able to understand and apply the principles of research and critically to analyse and evaluate the range of available evidence supports this goal. Ultimately these skills will contribute not only to the dissemination and implementation of research findings in clinical practice, but to the development of professional knowledge. This book will provide a valuable foundation.

Sonia Crow
Assistant Director for Educational Policy
(Research and Development)
English National Board
for Nursing, Midwifery and Health Visiting

ACKNOWLEDGEMENTS

We would like to acknowledge the students from our faculty who have undoubtedly made us think carefully and justify the importance of why nurses need an understanding of research. We would also like to recognize the influence of many qualified nurses in the local Trusts who have attended various research awareness courses organized by us. They have prevented us from making research awareness an academic exercise by keeping our feet firmly rooted in clinical practice and not allowing us to live in Cloud-cuckoo-land!

PREFACE

This book is intended for qualified nurses and students who have not had any opportunity to study or experience nursing research. It is a basic introductory text designed to be of practical use for the nurse of today. Our aim is to 'demystify' and explain research by introducing the essential elements relevant to the nursing profession.

The idea and motivation for the book came from our experience of teaching 'research awareness' to pre-registration nurses and qualified nurses on various courses. We were very aware of the need to make the topic of research as interesting as possible, and this included making it relevant for nursing practice. There are a number of similar introductory texts; however it is not always obvious whether they are aimed at potential nurse researchers or for general research awareness. This book is clearly aimed at giving qualified nurses and student nurses an introduction to research, with the expectation that those nurses wanting to carry out research will gain research training and read more in-depth and definitive texts to help them.

We have closely examined recommendations from the major reports published by the Department of Health regarding nursing and health service research, and follow the guidance that all nurses need to become research literate. We do this in the book by providing a foundation of research knowledge and a basis for critical evaluation of research. Through this knowledge, we hope to help nurses make sense of it all and enable them to become 'critical consumers of research'. This in turn will empower them to provide the highest standards of care for their patients and clients.

The layout of the book is straightforward and each chapter can be read on its own without the need to continually refer to other chapters. Following the first chapter that provides an overview of research in nursing, and Chapter 2 that discusses the nature of nursing knowledge, Chapters 3 to 9 explore the research process in some detail. Chapter 10 considers the often neglected area of ethics and nursing research, and Chapter 11 is a key chapter that considers critical evaluation of research. The final chapter looks into the future and contemplates the way forward for nursing research.

We have provided two appendices which we hope will be useful resources for nurses, and a glossary that defines appropriate research terms. Each chapter has learning outcomes, key terms and a list of suggested further reading. References to publications referred to in each chapter will be found towards the end of the book.

We hope that this book will make research interesting for nurses, and that it will stimulate further exploration of the subject. More importantly, our desire is to see nurses understanding research so that they can consider it in their daily practice. Patients and clients can benefit from nurses who are able to use research appropriately to provide the highest standards of care possible.

CHAPTER 1
The role of research in nursing

Learning outcomes

On completion of this chapter the reader should be able to
- understand the development of nursing research in the United Kingdom.
- appreciate the need to become research literate.
- identify the major reports influencing the recent development of British nursing research.
- consider different ways of defining research.

Key terms

definitions of nursing research   'Taskforce Strategy'
research literacy   *A Vision for the Future*

INTRODUCTION

The term 'research literate' has been used by many to describe the way that the professional nurse of today should be. This is a term that we favour, as our intention is not to encourage nurses to undertake research, but rather to become research literate by a greater understanding of research in nursing and the health services. This does not mean that we think nurses should not be undertaking research. To the contrary, many nurses are conducting research in the health services. What we believe is that in order to undertake research, it is necessary to possess particular skills and knowledge, and the majority of nurses do not have, nor need, these skills. What they do need, however, are the skills and knowledge to appreciate, understand and use research in order to provide the highest quality and most effective care possible for their patients and clients. It should become natural for nurses to rely on research findings and evidence in their daily work.

Nurses need to be able to gain access to relevant research and be able to read and critically evaluate research reports. This will enable them to assess the appropriateness of using specific research based evidence in their daily practice, and to identify research problems and priorities. Furthermore, if research is taking place in clinical areas, nurses need to be aware of any potential ethical issues that may arise in relation to patients and clients. This includes having an understanding of the implications of collecting data for other researchers.

Nursing care must be based on current knowledge and evidence that promotes the delivery of the highest standards of nursing care possible. Nursing is continually striving for professional status and this requires the profession to have a knowledge base with its foundations in research. Excellence in practice is dependent on the research base of the profession. This also means that individuals must take responsibility for keeping abreast of developments, including research within their own sphere of the profession.

Prior to the introduction of Diploma-level pre-registration education (Project 2000), research appreciation and understanding was limited in the curriculum. This means that there are many qualified nurses who have not had the opportunity to explore and become aware of nursing research. These nurses now recognize the need to become research literate and are seeking out opportunities to develop their understanding and awareness of research in the health service. There are many courses, study days, books and journal articles which are accessible to most nurses and will help in their understanding of research. Being able to attend a conference is also a good opportunity to become aware of clinically related research in nursing.

THE DEVELOPMENT OF NURSING RESEARCH

The history of nursing research is comparatively short when compared to other professions (Robertson, 1994). Florence Nightingale in the nineteenth century identified the need for observation in her studies of patient care, and the necessity of systematic collection of information and data. Her use of statistics in the organization of the nursing workforce and measuring the outcomes of nursing and medical care has been a major influence in developing nursing research. However, it was not until the 1940s that nursing research really began to develop. This may have been due partly to medical dominance over the nursing profession and the more advanced development of medical knowledge through research, and partly through the lack of power in the nursing profession. Nurses have been used to helping medical colleagues in their research, but not necessarily undertaking their own research or being an equitable member of a research team.

Nursing research can be linked to the advancement of nursing as a profession and the need for nursing theory and knowledge to under-pin clinical practice. The Report of the Committee on Nursing (Department of Health and Social Security, 1972) was the first major document to emphasize the importance of research in nursing. The Briggs Report, as it is commonly known, discussed the need to foster 'research-mindedness' in pre-registration training, and for further preparation in research for some nurses, midwives and health visi-tors. However, it was only through degree courses that nurses were systematically introduced to research during their basic training (Royal College of Nursing, 1982). In 1982, the Research Society of the Royal College of Nursing produced a short report called *Research-Mindedness and Nurse Education*. They re-emphasized the need for research-mindedness to be developed in all nurses, through nurse education programmes. This included a research based approach to patient care in written examination and assessments. However, it was not until the late 1980s and educational reforms such as Project 2000 that research based education and research awareness were systematically developed in pre-registration programmes of nursing.

A significant factor in the development of research awareness in the pre-registration curriculum is the closer link of nurse education with higher education. The emphasis is on research awareness, and it has been made clear that pre-registration students at Diploma level (Project 2000) should not be undertaking research but rather devel-oping critical enquiry and adopting an analytical approach to their practice: 'The programmes should encourage the spirit of specula-tive enquiry and enable students to gain an understanding of research methods and their use but not at a level to prepare them to undertake research' (English National Board, 1993, p. 3).

RECENT REPORTS

In recent years, a number of reports have been released which focus on the future of nursing, midwifery and health visiting. They have all had an influence on the nursing profession to varying degrees, and some have made a significant contribution with regard to nursing research. They are freely available from good nursing libraries or from their original source of publication. The remainder of this section on the development of nursing research will discuss some of the most important issues from these reports.

Research-mindedness and Nurse Education

This short report was produced by a working group of the Research Society of the Royal College of Nursing in 1982. It considered that during nurse training, nurses should develop an awareness of research findings, the implications of the findings for the care of patients, and that there may be a need for further questioning and research. The group used the term 'research-mindedness', which they defined as: '... a critical and questioning approach to one's work, the desire and ability to find out about the latest research in that area, and the ability to assess its value to the situation and apply it as appropriate' (Royal College of Nursing, 1982, p. 1).

Despite the date of publication, the central idea is reinforced by reports published over a decade later.

A Vision for the Future

A Vision for the Future was published by the Department of Health (Department of Health, 1993a). Its aim was to provide a considered view of the future for nurses, midwives and health visitors. In particular it concentrated on the way that nurses, midwives and health visitors could contribute to the National Health Service reforms. Twelve targets were identified, and of particular interest with regard to research are targets eight and nine.

Target eight
Professional leaders should, in partnership with academic departments and others, set the nursing, midwifery and health visiting research agenda and establish networks to disseminate practice informed by research findings ... *professional leaders*

should be able to demonstrate the existence of local networks to disseminate good practice based on research.

Target nine
Every nurse, midwife and health visitor should be able to recognise the role of research and research based knowledge in the delivery of high quality care ... *providers should be able to demonstrate at least three areas where clinical practice has changed as a result of research findings.* (p. 14)

The targets from *A Vision for the Future* have been accepted to varying degrees by Health Authorities and Trusts. Some Trusts have developed the targets into their own strategies for nursing, midwifery and health visiting, and evaluate the outcomes. In relation to target eight, for example, this could involve looking at the development of research interest groups and journal clubs, and monitoring their effect on patient care. With regard to target nine, this could include clinical auditing of the use of research evidence in the delivery of patient and client care.

Taskforce on the Strategy for Research in Nursing, Midwifery, and Health Visiting

The *Report of the Taskforce on the Strategy for Research in Nursing, Midwifery, and Health Visiting* was published in 1993 by the Department of Health. The Taskforce was set up in April 1992 to consider the role, potential and future development of nursing research. The Taskforce Strategy was set in the context of an overall research and development strategy for the National Health Service (Department of Health, 1993b) and recommended the integrating of nursing research into the wider domain of health services research. Although there was an argument for nursing research to be developed independently, the Taskforce considered full integration into health service research to be the most appropriate way forward. The Taskforce was very clear regarding the way forward with research education and training:

Research skills and experience need to be far more widespread than at present in the nursing professions, and the links between research and practice need to be much stronger. This does not mean that all practitioners should be carrying out research as part of their professional role or their professional development: indeed, the proliferation of inadequate unsupervised, small scale projects should be curbed. However, every practitioner does need to develop a capacity for critical thought and to acquire analytical skills; a smaller number – but far more than at present – require research training to enable them to engage in research while retaining their clinical base or to bridge the worlds of research decision-making, practice development and policy. A minority will make a career in full-time research. (Department of Health, 1993b, para. 3.31, pp. 12, 13)

The report goes on to discuss research literacy as an 'essential prerequisite of knowledge-led practice' (para. 3.32, p. 13). This is defined as having an understanding of the research process, the ability to retrieve and critically assess research, and the ability to define research problems and priorities.

The Taskforce Strategy has been well received within the nursing profession, and the many recommendations are being considered in relation to other policies and practice within the health service. The English National Board for Nursing, Midwifery and Health Visiting has been quick to respond to the Taskforce Strategy and outlines its response through a position paper (English National Board, 1994). It welcomes the Strategy and has made the following statements which seek to support the development of research appreciation and research skills within the professions by ensuring that:

- the content of the education programmes it approves is based wherever possible on research findings
- education programmes contain research appreciation
- research skills of nurses, midwives and health visitors involved in the education and training of students are further developed. (p. 2)

DEFINITIONS OF NURSING RESEARCH

There are many definitions of nursing research, ranging from very broad to very restrictive accounts of research. A quick look through the literature would reveal many different definitions. A broad definition might suggest that research is any type of inquiry that generates knowledge, and may include a variety of activities. Depoy and Gitlin (1994) favour a broad approach in their text, although they are not only concerned with nursing, but health and human services research. They define research as 'multiple, systematic strategies to generate knowledge about human behaviour, human experience, and human environments in which the thought and action process of the researcher are clearly specified so that they are logical, understandable, confirmable and useful' (p. 5). This is an interesting definition in that the role of the researcher is acknowledged as important. Many definitions of research do not consider this aspect.

Polit and Hungler (1995) define research as 'systematic enquiry that uses orderly scientific methods to answer questions or solve problems' (p. 652). This definition has a clear practical dimension in that research is seen to answer questions or solve problems. As with the Depoy and Gitlin (1994) definition, 'systematic' is a common theme and one which occurs in many other definitions.

Nursing is clearly linked with the social sciences and one definition of social research by Neuman (1994) may be of use to nurses:

> Social research involves many things. It is how a person finds out something new and original about the social world. To do this, a researcher needs to think logically, follow rules, repeat steps over and over. A researcher will combine theories or ideas with facts in a systematic way and use his or her imagination and creativity. (p. 2)

Two key themes that emerge from most definitions are the 'search for knowledge' and that the process is systematic and rigorous.

The Taskforce Strategy (Department of Health, 1993b) continues on with this idea of being methodical and systematic. However, it uses a much narrower definition of research: 'We use the term research to mean vigorous and systematic enquiry, conducted on a scale and using methods commensurate with the issue to be investigated, and designed to lead to generalisable contributions to knowledge' (para. 1.4.1, p. 6). By using a term such as 'generalisable' this definition is suggesting that a quantitative rather than qualitative approach to research is important. This debate about quantitative and qualitative approaches is developed further in Chapter 5.

For the purpose of this book, we define nursing research as:

> a systematic approach to gathering information for the purposes of answering questions and solving problems in the pursuit of creating new knowledge about nursing and nursing care.

The definition is broad in order to encompass all aspects of nursing and nursing care and it recognizes the systematic nature of collecting data. In addition, we consider the active, practical and applied nature of nursing. In order to distinguish research from audit and development work, which are closely related, we define research as creating new knowledge. No single definition will be satisfactory however, and in order to be able to understand research at an introductory level, we feel that a working definition is necessary. We will develop this discussion in some of the later chapters.

RESEARCHERS IN NURSING

There are many people who undertake research that could come under the broad category of 'nursing research'. At one end of the spectrum there are members of those disciplines such as psychology, sociology, social policy, who will examine nursing and nursing care from the perspective of their own discipline. At the other end are nurses who undertake research from a nursing perspective in order to make a direct improvement to patient care. In both groups there will be academic researchers who are in pursuit of knowledge. However, in the second group, there will also be nurses who are aiming to look directly at nursing practice and patient care. There may be research nurses directly employed in specialities such as breast care, respiratory nursing or paediatrics, who undertake small studies in their own area of work. Or there may be nurses employed directly onto a specific project, for example a clinical trial examining the effectiveness of a counselling service. A quick look at journals such as the *Journal of Advanced Nursing*, the *Journal of Clinical Nursing* or the *British Journal of Nursing* will give some ideas of the type of research that is conducted and reported by nurses.

The Department of Health are keen to take a multidisciplinary and collaborative approach to research in the health services. This includes teams with nurses, midwives and health visitors (Department of Health, 1993c). We are beginning to see evidence of this in the health service, and in some research projects, where a nurse is leading a multidisciplinary team.

There are also many nurses who are undertaking research as part of a course, or during a period of study. These may be undergraduate nurses, qualified nurses taking a first degree or Master's degree, or nurses studying at Doctoral level. As previously mentioned, nurses studying at Diploma level are not encouraged to undertake research, although they might carry out activities such as designing a questionnaire or interviewing colleagues as exercises to help them understand research methods. More commonly, they will learn to evaluate research critically in order to inform their nursing practice. Diploma students may also undertake project work or write essays using research findings and evidence. All these activities are important and necessary in helping nurses to become research literate. However, it is important to distinguish activities and projects from 'research' as previously defined as the 'creation of new knowledge'.

There are a number of organizations that will fund nursing-related research. The English National Board for Nursing, Midwifery and Health Visiting commissions and finances a number of projects that are related to education and practice. The Department of Health, the Medical Research Council and the Economic and Social Research Councils are also large organizations that will consider funding particular pieces of nursing research, or may commission research. Some charitable organizations, such as the Joseph Rowntree Foundation, the Nuffield Foundation and the Leverhulme Trust, will consider funding research related to nursing, and there are also many smaller organizations that may consider support.

THE NEED FOR NURSING RESEARCH

As nurses we want to be able to give the very best care to our patients and clients. In order to do this, we need to know what is the best and how to give it. Research findings and evidence can give us some of the knowledge to help us decide what is best and therefore deliver the highest standards of care possible. To be research literate, nurses need to be able to find and critically assess research evidence, and with those skills, explore ways in which effective research can be applied to practice. We therefore need to become critical consumers of research. In addition, all nurses need to be able to identify problems and research questions that have been generated from their clinical practice and knowledge of research. These questions may then initiate further research with a view to improving patient and client care.

Knowledge with a foundation in research evidence is essential for any profession. Current and continuing research also enables a profession to develop further. As a still developing profession, nursing has further to go than many other established professions. However, research awareness is firmly placed on the nursing curriculum, and practitioners are recognizing the need to become research literate.

Key points

- All nurses need to become research literate.
- Research literacy includes the skills and knowledge to appreciate, understand and use research.
- Not all nurses should be conducting research as part of their clinical role or professional development.
- There are many definitions of research, with most incorporating a view about the search for knowledge through a systematic and rigorous process.
- Nurses need to become critical consumers of research to enable them to provide excellence in nursing care.

FURTHER READING

Department of Health (1993a) *A Vision for the Future*. London: Department of Health.

Department of Health (1993b) *Report of the Taskforce on the Strategy for Research in Nursing, Midwifery and Health Visiting*. London: Department of Health.

Department of Health (1993c) *Research for Health*. London: Department of Health.

Department of Health (1994) *Testing the Vision: A Report on the Progress in the First Year of* A Vision for the Future. London: Department of Health.

Depoy, E. and Gitlin, L. N. (1994) *Introduction to Research: Multiple Strategies for Health and Human Services*, ch. 1. St Louis: Mosby.

English National Board for Nursing, Midwifery and Health Visiting (1994) *The Board's Response to the Strategy for Research*. London: English National Board for Nursing, Midwifery and Health Visiting.

Hardey, M. and Mulhall, A. (eds) (1994) *Nursing Research: Theory and Practice*, ch. 1. London: Chapman & Hall.

LoBiondo-Wood, G. and Haber, J. (eds) (1994) *Nursing Research: Methods, Critical Appraisal and Utilization*, 3rd edn, ch. 1. St Louis: Mosby.

Polit, D. and Hungler, B. (1995) *Nursing Research: Principles and Methods*, 5th edn, ch. 1. Philadelphia: J. B. Lippincott Co.

Reed, S. (1994) 'The Strategy for Research in Nursing in England: initial impact', *Nurse Researcher* 1(3), 72–84.
Reid, N. (1993) *Health Care Research by Degrees*, ch. 1. Oxford: Blackwell Scientific Publications.
Robertson, J. (ed.) (1994) *Clinical Nursing Research*, ch. 1. London: Churchill Livingstone.
Tierney, A. (1993) 'Research literacy: an essential prerequisite for knowledge-led practice', *Nurse Researcher* 1(1), 79–83.

CHAPTER 2
The nature of nursing knowledge

Learning outcomes

On completion of this chapter the reader should be able to
- identify the sources of knowledge available to nursing.
- appreciate the importance of scientific and research based knowledge for nursing practice.

Key terms

authority
common sense
intuition
reflective practice
rituals

scientific knowledge
sources of knowledge
traditions
trial and error

INTRODUCTION

Many nursing research texts fail to consider the development of nursing knowledge and practice, and the significance of scientific and research based information to the nature of nursing knowledge. It is the intention of this chapter to consider how nursing knowledge has developed, and to highlight the need for nursing to build its own body of information as part of professional growth.

In an attempt to understand the nature of nursing knowledge, the complexity of nursing information is discussed and the multidimensional aspects of nursing's theory base are considered. The development of knowledge through nursing tradition, ritualistic practice, intuition, common sense, authority, trial and error, other disciplines, and from a scientific base, will be included. Such discussions will reveal the many dimensions of nursing theory and, whilst not denigrating the development of any particular source of knowledge, will demonstrate the need for nursing to question its knowledge base and accept those sources that provide a credible base for practice.

TYPES OF KNOWLEDGE IN NURSING

As a professional discipline, nursing has needed to develop its own knowledge base. Such developments have been multidimensional, with knowledge being generated from many different sources. Before considering these in some detail it is important to examine the need for nursing to be supported by different types of knowledge.

It is generally accepted that nursing cannot be classified as either an art or a science, but is a profession which is bound in both fields. The science of nursing emphasizes the importance of scientific (empirical) knowledge within nursing. This has been described as 'know that' knowledge, knowing why you do something, having a rationale for your actions. This knowledge is open to scientific testing and systematic investigation, allowing for validation of theory. The art of nursing (aesthetic dimension) is more closely allied to the practice of nursing and is described as 'know how' knowledge, knowing what to do. This knowledge is developed through experience of nursing practice and is not easily tested or explained scientifically. Benner (1984) suggests the expert practitioner uses 'know how' knowledge developed through years of practising nursing skills. This knowledge cannot be scientifically justified, but is essential to expert practice.

The art and science of nursing was outlined by Carper (1978) who suggested that personal and ethical knowledge also exist within nursing. Personal knowledge is unique to the individual and is developed through personal experience and thought. Within nursing practice and education, the current development of reflective practice encourages the nurse to reflect on experience as a way of learning and developing. Ethical knowledge forms the basis of ethical and moral decisions, taken at times of dilemma.

Guilding (1993) applies empirical, aesthetic, personal and ethical dimensions of nursing knowledge to wound care. In this example, the empirical dimension of wound care would involve the practitioner using scientific knowledge of wound assessment, wound healing, wound care techniques and products in wound care. The aesthetic dimension would allow the practitioner to adapt the skill of applying wound-dressing materials to a particular wound using the principles of wound care appropriately, as opposed to following a set routine. The practitioner would use individual experience of wound care, thus applying personal knowledge, and follow competent practices in wound care, such as maintaining asepsis, to achieve the ethical dimension of nursing knowledge.

In applying different dimensions of nursing knowledge to wound care, some impression of the way in which different sources of knowledge inform nursing is given. The following paragraphs will consider the influences of different sources of knowledge in nursing, beginning with traditional and ritualistic origins.

TRADITIONS AND RITUALS

'We do it this way because we believe this is the best way.' 'We do it the way Sister likes it.' 'Dr X likes his patients to be treated in this particular way.' 'You watch me and learn how to do it.' These statements all reflect the use of tradition in nursing, the development of practice based on beliefs or myths which are accepted by the profession as a base for practice, as if they were facts. Traditions can become custom, applied without critical thought, in a ritualistic way. There are many examples within nursing. Spiller (1992) cites the morning bed bath or wash as a ritual, being given to patients regardless of need, desire, or the patient's usual washing practice. Toms (1993) discusses the taking of vital observations of blood pressure, temperature, pulse and respirations, as a ritual practice based in tradition and custom, rather than on individual assessment of need.

Walsh and Ford (1989) devote a text to the discussion of ritual practices in nursing, which is full of examples of care being given without thought for individual need. Walsh and Ford (1989) state: 'Nursing care is failing the patient because it is institution led rather than patient driven ... The cause of this failure, we suggest, is rooted in the traditional rituals and myths that still abound in the wards and departments of hospitals today.' The text gives a picture of the way in which traditions and rituals impinge on all aspects of the patient's day and demonstrates the use of outdated practice by many nursing staff. There is evidence to show that many practices are not questioned and problems are not approached in a logical and problem-solving way, but with a routine answer which can be based in unsubstantiated beliefs.

Walsh and Ford (1989) were not the first to consider ritualistic practice in nursing. Walker (1967) studied certain nursing practices and behaviours and concluded that not all practices which might be seen as ritualistic are necessarily undesirable. The performance of the ward report at shift changes acts as a vehicle for social exchange and enhances social cohesion. Wolf (1988) also identified the ward report as an occupational ritual which is a beneficial practice for the socialization of nurses into the nursing role. Holland (1993) concluded that the ward report is a ritual which 'reflects the values of nursing ... and ensures that common values enshrined in [nursing] practice are sustained'.

There are many practices in nursing that are based in tradition and ritual, and are performed in a routine way, using the same methods without question. Some such practices are thought to be beneficial to nursing and patient care, the example given being the ward report. It is, however, vital that outdated and unsafe practices are identified, to allow nurses confidence in the delivery of safe practice. Nursing cannot afford to perpetuate traditional and ritualistic practice if it is at the expense of developments which are beneficial to the patient and the profession. Nurses are accountable for their practice (United Kingdom Central Council for Nursing, Midwifery and Health Visiting, 1992) and must be able to identify that the best possible care is being made available, so that practice can be justified as the most appropriate.

INTUITION

The recognition of intuition as a source of nursing knowledge arises from recent developments within the profession, which is starting to acknowledge the importance of intuition as part of the decision-making process in nursing. The use of intuition is apparent in nursing practice, but cannot easily be explained. The nurse who knows what the patient's needs are without detailed assessment, who identifies the best way of treating an individual, who knows when a patient's life is at an end but cannot explain why this is known, uses intuitive knowledge. Intuition is perhaps having acute sensitivity, a sixth sense (Burnard, 1989), built on knowledge and experience which is applied to decision-making and problem-solving.

The lack of objectivity and ability to identify a rationale behind intuitive decisions has affected the recognition of this source of knowledge. Rew (1988) states: 'Few researchers in nursing acknowledge intuition as a valid and verifiable phenomenon for scientific investigation.' Yet, it is argued that there are many nursing situations where the application of intuitive knowledge is essential. These include the management of ethical dilemmas and situations where there is inadequate information with which to interpret potential behavioural response (Rew and Sparrow, 1987).

The experienced nurse brings additional sensitivity into nursing practice. This use of intuition enables the delivery of the best possible patient care. Benner (1984) sees the experienced nurse as the expert clinician who uses intuition as part of delivering holistic (total) care to the patient. Benner (1984) suggests 'know how' knowledge, which highlights the difference between the beginner or novice and the expert practitioner, should be valued more highly. The development of 'knowledge that' into 'knowledge how' as part of acquiring intuition allows the expert practitioner to view the complete situation and therefore apply holistic care, using past experience and knowledge. The value of intuition to holistic care is discussed by Agan (1987) who links intuitive knowledge to the development of personal knowledge through reflective practice.

Problem-solving through reflective practice was popularized by Argyris and Schon (1974), with the more recent work of Schon (1987) suggesting the development of two types of reflective skill. Reflection-in-action, where the nurse is appraising care and making change whilst practising, is compared with reflection-on-action which follows the event, using an analysis of preceding practice to shape the future.

The work of Schon (1987) has been influential in nursing practice and education, being adopted as a mode of learning within nurse education. Though the work has been criticized (Greenwood, 1993), the value given to reflective practice in building personal knowledge, and ultimately in developing intuition, confirms the place of intuitive knowledge as a potential source of nursing knowledge.

Intuitive knowledge is important in clinical decision-making and as part of delivering holistic care to patients. Rew (1988) suggests intuitive knowledge must be valued, and if acknowledged, methods which allow understanding of intuitive experiences will develop and facilitate the growth of these skills. It is important to ensure nursing encompasses intuitive knowledge in its existing knowledge base, to enable nurses to practise with both analytical and intuitive skill.

COMMON SENSE

To use the words 'common sense' is to suggest that something is widely accepted or generally known, as well as being logically reasoned and thought through. Common sense is the sort of thing that sensible people will usually do (Clark, 1987). Knowledge based on common sense is therefore gained through accepted understanding, developed through individual experience that is not associated with any formal education or training.

Its value as a source of nursing knowledge on which to base patient care is therefore limited, as can be seen through the examination of a common sense approach to certain clinical practices. Common sense might lead to covering a warm but shivering patient with extra blankets. Learned knowledge of the need to reduce a patient's temperature, and therefore the shivering, will result in the removal of any extra blankets and clothing. People often refer to bringing up children as common sense (Clark, 1987): 'Mr and Mrs Smith will be "good" parents because they have a lot of common sense.' While it may be true that Mr and Mrs Smith will be 'good' parents, there is nothing that is at all common about the approach to parenthood. This can be seen in the plethora of texts available for parents that offer differing advice on all aspects of child care.

As common sense is derived from individual experience, it is naturally limited, can be biased, and is drawn from individual reasoning rather than from external sources. The rationale for practice is consequently unsupported and may lead to the delivery of care which is not the best available, or the most appropriate.

Challenging practice based on common sense can be fraught with problems, as to the individual the practice is reasonable and understandable, to them it makes common sense. Questioning common sense is, however, necessary to ensure care is of a high standard, and to prevent the perpetuation of practices that are restricted by individual experience and bias.

Common sense can provide a useful approach to care delivery, but nurses, as accountable practitioners, must critically examine and evaluate practice, choosing a knowledge base which supports professional and quality care.

TRIAL AND ERROR

Most of us use trial and error in solving problems on a day-to-day basis. When presented with a problem we will try one way of resolving it, and if this fails, different approaches will be taken until a solution is found. The solution is then remembered and used if the same or similar problem occurs again.

Trial and error will only provide a solution to one specific problem and is therefore limited in its use. It is however an important source of knowledge, as solutions may be recommended for use by others faced with similar problems. For example, much advice is offered to people with common colds, such as to feed a cold, take high doses of vitamin C, eat boiled onions while soaking both feet in a hot mustard bath. The implications of passing on knowledge gained through trial and error learning may be to contribute to traditional knowledge or in fact to authoritative knowledge that is considered later.

Within nursing there are many practices that have been developed through trial and error. Wound care is one of the many areas where knowledge has been generated through trial and error. Cuzzell and Stotts (1990) present an appraisal of wound-care treatments which have developed through trying particular wound-care practices and products, and evaluating their usefulness.

The very nature of nursing education prior to the Diploma (Project 2000) course fostered a trial and error approach to learning. Students were part of the workforce, learned on the job, were often unsupervised and thus were left to resolve problems by working through a number of possible solutions.

Knowledge based on trial and error, which may ultimately be developed into traditional or authoritative knowledge, can provide a valid basis for care. The appropriateness of using such knowledge should, however, be established through systematic investigation, so that patients can be assured of the rationale behind the care they receive.

AUTHORITY

Knowledge originating from people in positions of authority, who are often perceived as experts, can be accepted as a reasonable basis for practice. There are many individuals who impart authoritative knowledge: specialist nurses, nurse managers, nurse teachers, medical staff, pharmacists, the clinical nurse who supervises the student. In fact all personnel in the health care environment have the potential to be seen as an authority. This may develop from the person's position, which is likely to be one of power, or from the person's perceived knowledge and experience, or from the very personality and self-portrayal of the individual.

As a source of knowledge, the expert may have much to offer that will benefit students, staff and ultimately patients. There is, however, a concern that the expert will not be challenged, that the position of authority is above reproach and that the knowledge of the expert can be used without questioning the source. It is possible for the expert to offer a vehicle for the perpetuation of traditional and ritualistic practice, of practices which support the expert's preference and idiosyncrasies, rather than practice which is in fact sound and based on fact. There are many examples of such practice. The teaching of cardio-pulmonary resuscitation has varied according to the individual demonstrating basic life support skills, and continues to vary despite the development of European Resuscitation Council Guidelines (European Resuscitation Council, 1992) that are based on current factual knowledge. It is therefore important for the recipient of authoritative knowledge to establish the original source of the information and determine a basis for practice that is justifiable.

It should also be remembered that experts impart knowledge through publication. The content of any journal article or text should not be accepted as true just because it is published, but it should be questioned and critically appraised. All health care professionals need critical reading skills to determine the strengths and weaknesses of published work, and should be encouraged to adopt a questioning approach.

Hospital procedures and policies are also used to guide nursing practice. Many procedures used in the past gave step-by-step instructions for the practitioner to follow. More recently, principles have replaced the procedural approach. These are less prescriptive and offer guidelines for safe practice. It is, however, important that the knowledge behind clinical principles is established. Rationales should be offered, which include referenced facts.

The practitioner needs to question authority as a source of knowledge in order to be confident in its use. The expert is not above reproach, but should offer facts rather than fiction to those who look for expert guidance.

THE CONTRIBUTION OF OTHER DISCIPLINES

As an emerging profession, nursing has only recently turned its attention to developing its own body of knowledge in any depth. This has allowed great influence from more established professions, whose theory has given direction to nursing practice. Historically, nursing was closely embroiled in medicine, with the 'medical model' providing a framework for nursing practice. The nursing curriculum was delivered by medical practitioners who used a disease-orientated approach and medical diagnosis as the basis for nursing practice. The nurse's role was to carry out the doctor's orders and meet the needs of the medical profession.

The powerful presence of medicine is now challenged, and though the need for knowledge of human science continues, acknowledgement of the health and social sciences is seen. The art and science of nursing encompasses a wide knowledge base, which is generated from many sources, such as sociology, psychology, pharmacology, medicine, law, ethics, ergonomics, to name but a few. Nursing is also concerned to generate its own unique body of knowledge and to test existing sources; thus the need for scientific knowledge in nursing is established.

SCIENTIFIC KNOWLEDGE

Scientific knowledge is seen as informing nursing through solving problems in a logical, systematic and rigorous way. The scientific approach to generating knowledge is 'the most sophisticated method of acquiring knowledge that humans have developed' (Polit and Hungler, 1993). Chapter 1 gave some of the many definitions of research, which share commonality in suggesting a systematic approach to testing and generating knowledge. This suggests that the research process, described in Chapter 3, is used to provide logical and systematic structure to problem-solving.

The need for scientific knowledge is acknowledged in the opening chapter, as is the need for education and training to enable nurses to develop research awareness skills. Such skills are necessary to analyse critically and appraise research, thus allowing the identification of strengths and weaknesses in the research process.

The need for the nursing profession to develop a scientific knowledge base for practice is also established, with research being viewed as a professional necessity. Research is vital for the development of cost-effective and credible care, which can be delivered confidently by the accountable practitioner (Ashworth, 1985; cited in Hawthorn, 1985). There are obvious and undisputed benefits for the patient and profession in developing research based nursing practice. In fact, the discussions in this chapter have highlighted the need to challenge the very nature of nursing knowledge; to question the traditions and rituals, the expert, common sense, trial and error, and intuition borne of experience. Only through appraisal of the information used to support nursing practice, will the professional nurse be able to offer justification for nursing care and provide informed rationale for practice.

Consideration is needed, however, in the development of both the science and art of nursing, and indeed the personal and ethical dimensions of nursing. Earlier in the chapter the difficulties in measuring 'knowledge how' were identified. The art of nursing and application of care cannot easily be measured using a scientific research approach. For example, if the practice of giving injections were considered, it would be possible to measure certain aspects of technique scientifically. Using a quantitative approach as described in Chapter 5, it would be possible to study the best injection sites, the best equipment to use, and other aspects of the injection technique. However, if the personal and aesthetic knowledge were to be ascertained, then a qualitative approach (see Chapter 5) might identify the nurses' feelings before, during and after giving injections, and consider how these feelings were believed to affect injection techniques. Quantitative research may be used to test a research question or hypothesis about injection technique, whereas the qualitative approach may be applied to find out how nurses feel about the practice of injection technique. The development of nursing knowledge must encompass the definitions of nursing as an intellectual, theoretical, and practice based profession. Research must therefore support measurement and testing of knowledge in a systematic way, whilst facilitating the development of the art of nursing and building theories which enhance nursing practice.

As well as testing the boundaries of research, the development of scientific knowledge in nursing has its difficulties and limitations. Just as nurses need to be critical in their appraisal of other sources of knowledge, so they need to be critical of research. The strengths and weaknesses of scientific knowledge must be identified through critical reading, as is highlighted in Chapter 11. No research is infallible, all will have both strengths and limitations which should be considered in evaluating any of the recommendations made for practice.

The very nature of nursing causes research difficulties, including ethical problems and measurement issues. Certain research may not gain ethical approval. For example, testing the development of pressure areas would be limited by existing knowledge, which any further research would have to acknowledge. Research that proposed leaving patients for longer than two-hour periods before pressure area assessment, ignores current knowledge and would endanger the patient. Such research would be seen as negligent and unethical.

Though there are many measurement tools available to the researcher (see Chapter 8), the measurement of quality information, as part of a qualitative approach, poses difficulties. The measurement of opinions, feelings, thoughts, viewpoint, behaviour, can challenge research. In fact, Polit and Hungler (1993) suggest 'problems associated with measurement are the most perplexing in the research process'.

Additional difficulties lie in nursing itself. The impetus for research is uncertain, the education and research skills of the profession need developing, and there is no uniform application of research knowledge to practice. Nursing does not have an established research background, which leads to difficulties of recognition in research fields. Castledine (1994) suggests nurses are not seen as credible researchers, so are not viewed favourably by those funding research. Only time will tell if research funds are more readily obtained as nursing moves into academia, as part of the integration of nurse education into universities.

Even when established in higher education, nurses will need to acquire research knowledge and skills to shape the future of research. These are now developed to a basic level within pre-registration education, as part of Diploma (Project 2000) courses. Most post-registration courses include research awareness skills and there are a few specialized research courses for trained nurses. Some funding and support is also available for those nurses who choose to study and/or make a career in research, gaining higher research degrees and undertaking research at Doctorate level. These specific developments are reinforced by the Department of Health, *Report of the Taskforce on the Strategy for Research in Nursing, Midwifery and Health Visiting* (1993b), which seeks to reduce small-scale local research, to increase research awareness in nursing, and support the development of some research specialists.

It is hoped that the development of research awareness in nursing will improve the application of research knowledge to practice. It is known that some nurses are reluctant to use research findings in practice. Hunt (1981) is one author to comment, suggesting nurses are reluctant to use research because they don't know about it, they don't believe it, they don't understand it, don't see the relevance of it, and are not supported in making changes to practice. There are many examples of outdated practices that are perpetuated, despite scientific evidence that supports change. One example is the starvation of patients before surgery, which continues to occur from midnight for a morning theatre list, or six in the morning for an afternoon theatre list. This ignores knowledge supporting a more individual approach to fasting, with a suggested maximum four-hour period of withholding food (Hamilton-Smith, 1972). It also supports ritualistic practice and denies the patient individualized care.

It is important that nursing develops its own theory and tests existing sources of knowledge, so that nurses as accountable practitioners are able to justify nursing care and give a rationale for nursing actions. Scientific knowledge may not always be the most appropriate source of information on which to base practice, but the use of scientific enquiry will establish the best basis for nursing care.

Key points

- The development of nursing theory has been multi-dimensional, with knowledge being generated from many sources.
- Nursing cannot be classified as an art or a science, but embodies both fields.
- The development of nursing knowledge must encompass the definitions of nursing as an intellectual, theoretical and practice based profession.
- Research must support measurement and the testing of knowledge in a systematic way, whilst facilitating the development of the art of nursing and building theories which enhance nursing practice.
- There is still some reluctance within the profession to accept the importance of research and make appropriate change.

FURTHER READING

Benner, P. (1984) *From Novice to Expert: Excellence and Power in Clinical Nursing Practice*. California: Addison-Wesley.

Carper, B. (1978) 'Fundamental patterns of knowing in nursing', *Advances in Nursing Science* 1(1), 13–23.

Clark, E. (1987) *Sources of Nursing Knowledge*, Research Awareness Series, Module 2. London: Distance Learning Centre, South Bank University.

Nicoll, L. (ed.) (1992) *Perspectives on Nursing Theory*, 2nd edn. Philadelphia: J. B. Lippincott Co.

Robinson, K. and Vaughan, B. (1992) *Knowledge for Nursing Practice*. Oxford: Butterworth Heinemann.

Walsh, M. and Ford, P. (1989) *Nursing Rituals: Research and Rational Actions*. Oxford: Heinemann Nursing.

CHAPTER 3
Overview of the research process

Learning outcomes

On completion of the chapter the reader should be able to
- identify the stages of the research process.
- understand the inter-relationships between the stages of the research process.
- appreciate how the research process guides research activity.

Key terms

qualitative approach
quantitative approach
research process

INTRODUCTION

This chapter offers a broad overview of the stages which comprise the research process and discusses the functions of the research process, highlighting its use as a framework for research activity. In doing so, this chapter provides the basis to many of the chapters that follow, where issues raised will be further explored.

The research process is a framework which enables researchers to start with a problem and follow a series of logical stages, to end with an outcome or result (see Table 3.1). It is a theoretical model which, when applied by researchers, may not be followed in a sequential way. This can be likened to the nursing process which follows stages of assessment, planning, implementation and evaluation. It is unlikely that in applying the nursing process, the stage of assessment would be completed before planning commences. Assessment is likely to continue throughout the period of patient care, overlapping with the other stages of the nursing process. The same is true of the research process, which, though referred to as a list of stages from identifying the problem to interpreting the results, is not likely to be approached in such a linear way. It is more likely that some stages of the process would run concurrently, interrelate and interchange, and some may be completely omitted. For example, the research question may be formulated initially and then redefined or completely rewritten as the researcher has an opportunity to reflect on the progress of the research study.

In undertaking a research study, the researcher's progression through the research process would depend on the research approach taken, which can be qualitative (inductive) or quantitative (deductive). Qualitative approaches tend to be considered as less scientific, with the outcomes being achieved without the use of statistical measures, although some qualitative approaches do include some degree of statistical analysis (see Chapter 5). In contrast, the quantitative approach relies on statistical measures for its results and therefore necessitates the use of larger samples and more structured data collection tools (Polit and Hungler, 1993).

Reflection by the researcher at each stage of the research process can be considered beneficial to the ultimate outcomes of the research. At each stage of the research process the researcher may make alterations to the continuation of the study based on progressive evaluations and thus hope to improve the final outcome and results.

Many writers, such as Burnard and Morrison (1990), consider the research process from an operational perspective. They discuss how to use the research process to write a research proposal (a plan of proposed work completed by a researcher prior to undertaking research). In particular, they describe how to plan and carry out a research project, and finally consider how to present the research findings.

For most nurses, the research process provides a basis for evaluating completed research in a critical way, as is further discussed in Chapter 11. Knowledge of the stages of the research process therefore enables nurses to read research reports. This is facilitated as the research process is used by researchers to structure the literary presentation of research findings.

Table 3.1 Stages of the research process

- Identifying problems
- Searching the literature
- Critically reading research
- Setting research aims, questions and hypotheses
- Sampling techniques
- Data collection
- Data analysis
- Interpretation of results

IDENTIFYING PROBLEMS

The first stage in the research process is to define a problem. The research problem may be generated at a local level, by nurses experiencing or observing a particular problem in nursing. Research problems may also result from the identification of research priorities by, for example, the Department of Health, which funds specific research studies into problems such as cancers. Research may also be funded by charitable or private bodies, such as pharmaceutical companies.

The researcher can be considering research problems which pertain to local, national or international issues, and may be working alone or as part of a research team. Whatever the scale of the research, the researcher must be clear about the relevance of researching the identified problem and have a clear understanding of the purpose of the research. In other words, what is the research trying to achieve, what are the outcomes hoping to show, and how will they be used?

Whatever the purpose of the research, the research problem needs to be researchable. The researcher would need to consider how the problem can be investigated, what type of results are likely to be generated and how they would be analysed. In addition, the researcher needs to address any ethical issues, such as whether patients are involved in the investigation.

The research problem is often broad and requires some refinement to form research aims, questions and hypotheses (see later discussions and Chapter 6). This is achieved by further exploration of the problem area, which includes searching and reading relevant literature.

SEARCHING THE LITERATURE

Having identified the research problem, the researcher must undertake a literature search before refining the problem. The literature search involves the retrieval of literature which is relevant to the research problem. The literature search should continue throughout the period of the research study, to facilitate the use of any relevant literature published during the study period. However, the main literature search is likely to take place in the early stages of the research process.

The approach taken to searching the literature is important, as this affects the breadth and depth of literature obtained. A literature search which has not been thorough may lead the researcher wrongly to assume that there is no relevant literature available.

The literature search needs to be structured around key areas, perhaps starting with key concepts or words, and should progress systematically, with the original research problem providing the continued focus for the search. The researcher may be tempted by different lines of enquiry as the search continues, so must avoid diversions which have no relevance to the study.

There are many aids to searching literature available; these are fully discussed in Chapter 4. It is important that the researcher has sufficient knowledge and skills to access the resources. In addition, the researcher should use a reference or database system, recording details of literature that has been obtained or is likely to be accessed during the study. These records will be used throughout the study and may be of use in the future, particularly if further research is undertaken.

As well as researchers, all nurses need to be able to undertake a literature search. Literature searching skills are important for nurses as professionals. Such skills will facilitate the development of practice, supporting the acquisition and updating of knowledge. This is essential for the development of research based practice and, ultimately, quality care. Nurses undertaking further courses will also need to use literature searching skills to meet coursework requirements.

CRITICALLY READING RESEARCH

The reading of research literature often occurs concurrently with the literature search. However, the two stages are discussed separately to highlight fundamental differences between the two. The review of the research literature requires the use of critical analysis skills to determine the strengths and weaknesses of the research, whereas the literature search is used to identify the literature for review.

The process of critical review requires knowledge of the research process and can be assisted by the use of a framework, outlining the stages of critical analysis (see Appendix 2). Critical reading skills used in the process of critical review are discussed in Chapter 11. These skills are essential to the researcher and of importance to all nurses. If nursing care is to be developed from an objective and scientific base, nurses must have the skills needed to analyse nursing literature and offer an objective evaluation of research outcomes.

In reviewing the literature critically, the researcher may obtain the answer to the research problem, negating the need for further research. Alternatively, the need for further research may be confirmed, and suggestions as to how the study should progress may be gained. For example, the research methodology could be replicated, or the data collection tool could be reproduced for use in the study.

SETTING RESEARCH AIMS, QUESTIONS AND HYPOTHESES

The research aims, questions and hypothesis give focus and direction to the research study. The research aim, or aims, outline what the research study is hoping to achieve. The research question is developed following the literature review, and narrows the original problem into a more concise statement which is generally measurable.

The research hypothesis gives even greater focus to the research, as it offers a prediction of the anticipated research outcomes. The hypothesis is a statement that is tested by the researcher, and, depending on the findings, will either be accepted or rejected. Fuller explanations of this are given in Chapter 6.

SAMPLING TECHNIQUES

Sampling involves the collection of information on which decisions can be made and conclusions drawn. The selection of a sample is therefore a very important part of the research process. Before a sample is selected the researcher identifies the target population, which includes the entire membership of the group in which the researcher is interested and from which information can be collected.

The target population could include subjects or incidents. For example, the researcher may be interested in obtaining information from community nurses. All community nurses would therefore form the target population.

It is unlikely that the researcher would collect information from the entire target population, but a sample would be selected to take part in the study. The most important feature of sampling is the degree to which the sample represents the target population. For the sample to be truly representative, the subjects need to reflect the target population in as many ways as possible. If the target population are student nurses following the Adult Branch, the sample needs to be made up of students in the Adult Branch. Limitation of difference between the target population and sample is achieved to some degree through the use of accepted sampling techniques.

Sampling techniques fall into two sampling strategies, probability and non-probability sampling. Probability sampling reflects the use of random selection, with every member of the target population having an equal chance of being included in the sample. Different probability sampling techniques include simple, stratified, systematic and cluster sampling. Non-probability samples are selected without the use of random selection. The inclusion of subjects can be through convenience, quota, purposive and snowball sampling techniques. Individual sampling techniques are discussed in Chapter 7.

RESEARCH APPROACHES

The research design offers a plan of how the research will proceed. It includes consideration of the research approach which is to be taken and the research methods, data collection tools and the methods of data analysis that are to be employed.

The research design can favour quantitative (deductive) or qualitative (inductive) approaches to the research (see Chapter 5). This will be reflected in the sample size used, data collection method and techniques employed, and will be most evident in the results obtained and their analysis.

A pilot study is used as part of the research design, to check sampling techniques, to test the validity and reliability of data collection tools and to allow the researcher to practise research skills, such as interviewing techniques.

Reflection on the experiences gained during the pilot study will be used by the researcher to refine aspects of the main study. This can afford financial benefits and facilitates the effective use of resources in the final research study.

DATA COLLECTION TECHNIQUES

The researcher's choice of data collection instrument is influenced by the research approach taken. For example, a quantitative approach may be supported by structured data collection techniques, such as a questionnaire, whereas a qualitative approach may include the use of unstructured interviews or observational techniques.

The most commonly used techniques include physiological and psychological measures, measuring scales, questionnaires, interviews, observations and documentary evidence (see Chapter 8).

DATA ANALYSIS

The method of data analysis used will depend on the research approach taken and the method of data collection employed. To facilitate analysis, the results, often described as raw data, will be processed in some way.

Raw data generated through quantitative approaches tend to be numerical. Analysis of numerical data is often achieved using computer packages. Statistical tests are applied to the raw data to generate statistical results that are interpreted by the researcher (see Chapter 9).

Research which follows qualitative approaches generates data which are not amenable to statistical analysis, and it is the content of the results that is important. The analysis may begin during the stage of data collection, as the researcher can begin to identify trends or themes whilst gathering information.

INTERPRETATION OF RESULTS

The final stage of the research process includes interpretation of the results, formulation of conclusions and communication of the research findings to the nursing and health care professions. Interpretation of the findings occurs in the light of the original research aims, questions and any hypotheses made, whilst reflecting on previous research studies identified in a critical review of the literature.

Discussions should highlight the researcher's interpretations of the results, acknowledge any limitations of the research process and consider the generalizability of the results (can the results from the sample be applied to a target population?). The relevance and significance that the research findings might have for practice and research would also be implied from the research findings. For example, a change in existing nursing practice may be recommended, or suggestions for further research may be made.

Finally, the research findings must be communicated to any sponsors or funding body and the nursing profession. Thus the research study will increase the body of nursing and health care knowledge and contribute to the improvement of nursing practice. The research process is used as a framework for presentation, which can occur locally by the production of a research dissertation, through local research journal publications, research clubs and interest groups. Wider communication of the results can be achieved through publication in national journals and presentation of papers at conferences. Further discussions on the dissemination of research are included in Chapter 12.

Key points

- The research process is a framework which enables researchers to start with a problem and follow a series of logical and sequential steps, to end with an outcome or result.
- The research process includes the following stages: identifying the problems; searching the literature; critically reading research; setting research aims, questions and hypotheses; sampling techniques; data collection; data analysis and interpretation of results.
- Research problems can be generated locally or identified as research priorities by government, charitable or private bodies.
- Understanding the research process enables nurses to identify and read research studies.

FURTHER READING

Criss, E. (1993) 'The research process demystified', *Journal of Emergency Medical Services* 18(3), S-43–6.

LoBiondo-Wood, G. and Haber, J. (eds) (1994) *Nursing Research: Methods, Critical Appraisal and Utilization*, 3rd edn, ch. 4. St Louis: Mosby.

McNeill, P. (1990) *Research Methods*. London: Routledge.

Parahoo, K. and Reid, N. (1988) 'Research skills: the research process', *Nursing Times* 84(40), 67–70.

Polit, D. and Hungler, B. (1993) *Essentials of Nursing Research: Methods, Appraisal and Utilization*, 3rd edn, ch. 2. Philadelphia: J. B. Lippincott Co.

Schmitt, M. (1986) 'The research process versus related processes', *Oncology Nursing Forum* 13(4), 125–31.

CHAPTER 4
Searching and reviewing the literature

Learning outcomes

On completion of the chapter the reader should be able to
- appreciate the need for the nurse to develop literature searching skills.
- define the term 'literature search'.
- define the term 'literature review'.
- identify sources of nursing research.
- identify the steps in undertaking a literature search.
- understand the need to record accurately and store references.

Key terms

abstract   literature review
index   literature search

INTRODUCTION

Finding and retrieving literature is an essential skill for the nurse of today. As highlighted previously, nurses need to become research literate and this includes having the ability to search for, retrieve and critically assess literature. This chapter considers how nurses can find and retrieve literature. This is commonly known as literature searching. The chapter will also consider literature reviewing in general terms, and a later chapter will consider critical assessment of literature.

It is fairly obvious that researchers need to know their subject

Table 4.1 Reasons for a researcher to undertake a literature search

- To become familiar and knowledgeable about other studies and relevant reports in a particular subject area.
- To gather ideas about appropriate research methodology for their own study, e.g., sample, methods, analysis.
- To see if there are similar studies which could be replicated or refined (with permission).
- To see if the research question has already been answered.
- To enable the researcher to become more focused.
- To assist the researcher in refining the research problem, subject or topic of interest into a clear and specific research question, aim or hypothesis.

before embarking on a new piece of research. As Chapter 3 highlighted, in the early stages of the research process it is usual for a researcher to undertake a literature search at the commencement of a study, and also keep updating the search throughout the life of the study. The reasons for a researcher to undertake a literature search are multiple (see Table 4.1). They include the need to develop the research proposal by getting ideas about methodology, and the ability to extend the researcher's knowledge about the subject.

The majority of nurses are not going to be undertaking research themselves, but they do need to be able to undertake a literature search for a number of reasons (see Table 4.2).

Any nurse embarking on a course today is likely to find literature searching to be an essential skill to develop and become proficient in. The full range of nursing related courses from pre-registration through post-registration courses, and studying at degree level, would all require the skills of literature searching. As important as education, being able to search the literature effectively is essential for practice. Chapter 2 identifies ways in which we know things, and points out that these are not always accurate or satisfactory. Finding literature to support us is one way of developing our knowledge of a subject, and, as Abbott (1993) puts it, 'knowing the literature is a central element to the proper practice of nursing, health visiting and midwifery' (p. 19).

Table 4.2   Reasons for a nurse to undertake a literature search

- To become familiar and knowledgeable about a particular subject.
- To keep abreast of new research and development in a particular subject area.
- As part of academic assessment, coursework or project work.
- As necessary background work prior to setting standards and developing policy.
- As essential for developing knowledge and practice in relation to the highest quality of care that can be offered to patients and clients.

THE LITERATURE SEARCH

A literature search is a process by which a person looks for literature on a specific subject or topic. It needs to be undertaken in a systematic way, and requires time, determination and perseverance. A number of steps can be followed, and it can be helpful for the novice at literature searching to work through these (see Table 4.3).

The first stage is to locate suitable libraries. There are likely to be a few libraries that you could use. Libraries situated in colleges and universities where there is a nursing department are likely to have some useful resources. There may also be libraries provided by local Trusts or Health Authorities. These may be specifically for nurses, or more commonly a section in a medical or post-graduate medical library. You will have access to most of these local libraries. However, it is important to check what facilities you are allowed to use. If you are a student, you will have direct access to the college or university library and probably limited access to local Health Authority and Trust libraries. A qualified member of staff is likely to have access to the local library, but, unless they are on a course, limited access to college and university libraries. If a library provides a service in subjects such as psychology, biology, sociology, health etc., there will be an even wider choice. Finding a suitable library is an essential first stage in searching the literature.

SOURCES OF LITERATURE

Having found a suitable library, the next stage is to become familiar with the variety of sources of literature. These can be loosely

Table 4.3   Steps in undertaking a literature search

- Locate suitable libraries with the necessary facilities to meet your needs.
- Become familiar with the variety of sources of literature.
- Become familiar with the range of 'searching facilities' available to you, e.g., indexes, abstracts and current awareness publications.
- Identify keywords to help you methodically and thoroughly search through abstracts and indexes either manually or using CD-ROM or a combination.
- Obtain the reports and articles which you want to read critically.
- Record the full details and reference of the article or report including the source.

categorized into books, reports, journals, and bibliographic aids. Books will only have limited use if the reader is looking for the very latest research. They are useful for their coverage of a subject in some depth. However, it usually takes a while to get a book published, so it may be a little out of date before it reaches the bookshelves. This may not be important for some readers and for some subjects, but from a research point of view, usually the most recent work is necessary. Some edited books contain recent research on a particular topic, and these can be fairly up-to-date resources.

Reports are another useful resource to know about. There is a wide range of types of report, ranging from government reports, through to short reports written for the funders of research. Theses and dissertations that are written by students completing a piece of research for coursework can also be useful reports to look at.

The most important sources of research literature are the academic and professional journals. Some journals contain original research articles; these are known as primary journals. Secondary journals contain summaries or reviews of research. There are also many journals that publish a mixture of primary and secondary papers. Many journals contain a combination of original research papers, reviews and other articles such as care studies, discussion papers and news items. Appendix 1 lists some of the most commonly available journals, along with other sources of research literature.

Most academic and professional journals have a panel of referees who will receive papers from a journal editor prior to publication. They are asked by the editor anonymously to review the article, and send back comments to the editor who will then decide whether or not to publish the article. Referees are usually experts in a particular field, and will only look at papers in their own area of expertise. The credibility of a journal is in part dependent on the quality of the refereeing. From a reader's point of view, however, just because an article has been 'peer reviewed' or refereed, does not guarantee accuracy or good evidence. The reader will need critically to assess each article themselves in order to evaluate its use in clinical practice (see Chapter 11).

UNDERTAKING A LITERATURE SEARCH

Having become familiar with the range of resources available, the next stage in the literature searching process is to search in a systematic and methodical manner. Most articles and reports will be located by using bibliographic aids such as indexes and abstracts. Indexes and abstracts help you find references to articles and reports under a particular subject or topic.

Indexes list references to articles and papers from a predetermined range of journals and publications. The references are listed under alphabetical subject headings and the most useful indexes for nurses are: *The International Nursing Index*; *The Cumulative Index to Nursing and Allied Health Literature* (CINAHL); *Index Medicus*; *The Nurses and Midwives Index* (NMI); and *The Nursing Bibliography*, from the Royal College of Nursing. Abstracts are also listed in alphabetical subject headings, but they also contain a short abstract or summary with each entry. The most commonly available abstracts are *The Health Service Abstracts*, *Social Services Abstracts*, and *Nursing Research Abstracts*. Some libraries also subscribe to Current Awareness publications which fulfil a similar function to indexes but may be more up to date. Useful Current Awareness publications are: *Palliative Care Index*; *Complementary Medicine Index*; *British Institute of Learning Disabilities* (bild); and *Ethnic Minorities Health*.

In order to use the indexes and abstracts, you will need to identify keywords e.g., infection. The keyword is a word, or words, that is likely to have been used by the author in the title or content of articles or reports. You look up the keyword in the books of indexes or abstracts, or you can undertake a computerized search using 'compact disk read only memory' (CD-ROM). Some of the indexes, such as *The Cumulative Index to Nursing and Allied Health Literature* (CINAHL), are also published as databases in compact disc format for use on CD-ROM. *The International Nursing Index* and *Index Medicus* are also available as a compact disc called 'Medline'. There are also some other databases available on CD-ROM such as ERIC (education), CRIB (current research), ASSIA (applied social sciences), COCHRANE (pregnancy and childbirth), RCN CD-ROM and HealthPlan (health care planning, finance, management, manpower etc.). It is usual practice for a library to subscribe to a number of databases, and they can easily tell you what they have available. A few small libraries may do the search for you; however, this has limitations if you are not sure about what you are looking for and want to explore the literature for yourself, and perhaps alter the scope of the search. More useful would be to have either individual or group tuition on the use of CD-ROM, which is offered by most libraries, and this will then enable you to undertake your own searches.

To a certain extent, it is up to an individual as to whether they undertake a manual search, using the indexes and abstracts, or undertake a computerized search. For many people, a combination of manual and computerized searching is the most effective. However, a computerized search can be much quicker once you have mastered the skills of using CD-ROM, and you can print out the references, look at them on the screen, or download them on to a floppy disk for later examination. You will also find that a computerized search can generate literally hundreds of references, many of which will not be suitable. The computer allows you easily to refine the keyword by linking it with others, e.g., infection and hospital, and also confining the search to particular dates, or only United Kingdom publications. This allows you to be really selective in what references you want to examine rather than gather an abundance of irrelevant material.

The selection of keyword(s) is crucial, and the success of the search can be dependent on choosing an appropriate word(s). It is often a difficult task, which involves lateral thinking, imagination and, according to Burnard (1993), 'a certain amount of experimentation' (p. 59). The keyword is also dependent on the indexers who choose certain words to describe the content of a particular article. Some of the databases used on CD-ROM are American (for example CINAHL), and therefore the spelling of the keyword, or the terminology used, may be different, for example Odour/Odor, Labour/Labor, Stoma/Ostomy. There are lists of subject headings that may help in the selection of keywords; even more useful is looking at a thesaurus to find similar words or a synonym that could be used in the search.

Once the relevant articles and papers have been identified and noted from the search, they need to be obtained. In large libraries, you may be able to find and photocopy the article you want. If not, the article can be ordered for you, for which you may have to pay. When you have obtained the articles and papers you want, it is essential to make a full record of the details. This should include author, date of publication, title of article and title of journal, volume, issue and page numbers. Some articles contain all these details on the first page; for those that do not, it is useful to write these details on the front of the photocopied article. This will save a lot of wasted time later when you are trying to find the full details of the reference.

STORING REFERENCES

It is very useful, and often necessary, to develop a system for storing the references that you obtain. This could be a simple card filing system with references recorded on separate cards, and some form of index. Alternatively, you can develop a system on the computer that could easily be examined. Specific computer programs for storing references can be purchased e.g. Papyrus, Endnote Plus; these can be extremely useful as they allow you to use the stored references in different ways. For example, you can print out a list of your selected references in a variety of different styles, such as the Harvard or Vancouver system. Another way of storing references on a computer is to use a database program which is suitable for your computer.

Whichever way you choose to store the references that you have obtained, you always need certain information for each one. This includes the author's name and initials, year of publication, title of article, title of book or journal, volume number, issue number and page numbers, publisher, place of publication and edition number if a book. Many people also find it worthwhile to make a few notes about each of the references stored. This might include a few key-words, or where the reference was obtained, or an abstract of the article, or just general notes. Both card systems and computerized systems allow you to do this.

There are a number of other useful things that you can do in addition to manual and computerized searching. First, if you can obtain a few principal articles by experts in the field, you can trace some of the useful looking references that they have used. You may find that there are relevant studies that you have missed or that some studies are cited frequently. Another useful thing is to see if anybody has written a literature review on your subject or a related area. This will often be a fairly extensive critical review, and again can lead you to some useful references that you could pursue. It is also important to look at the contents page of back copies of journals that cover articles related to your subject. This is because the indexes and abstracts previously mentioned may not cover articles published in the past six months or so, although Current Awareness publications may be more up to date. Therefore, going through the latest issues of relevant journals or Current Awareness publications might pick up any literature that you may have missed and also familiarize you with the latest current issues. You may also get more ideas of different key-words that you could use in your computerized or manual search.

LITERATURE REVIEW

A literature review is a written piece of work that examines and summarizes a particular subject in some detail. It may be a large article or paper published as a literature review, or it may be a shorter piece that is found at the beginning of a research article. A literature review can perform a number of functions. It may describe what is written about a particular subject or topic. This might be an uncritical summary that identifies relevant material about the subject. More important, however, is a critical literature review, where the reviewer has systematically searched for relevant literature on a particular topic, and then critically evaluated each article or paper (see Chapter 11). The author then puts together all the evidence and arguments from these papers, and writes it up as a critical but balanced review.

In order to undertake a critical literature review, the reviewer needs skills to undertake a comprehensive literature search as well as skills of evaluation. Therefore, knowledge of research methods is essential as well as knowledge of the subject. All nurses need to develop skills to enable them to undertake a literature review. Most academic assignments expect some critical review of literature, and, for nurses in practice, a literature review may form the basis of setting a standard or developing guidelines for good practice or for auditing purposes. For the researcher, a critical literature review is essential for informing the research approach and methods of investigating the research question. It is an essential stage in any research process. Mason (1993) provides a very readable guide to the process of doing a literature review (pp. 43–55).

Key points

- All nurses need to develop literature searching skills.
- Searching for literature is a planned and methodical process with a number of key stages.
- There are numerous sources of literature, including journals, reports and books.
- Developing a system for storing references may be helpful.
- Indexes and abstracts can help locate relevant literature.
- Undertaking a thorough literature search requires time, energy and perseverance.

FURTHER READING

Abbott, P. (1993) 'Why do we need to review literature?', *Nurse Researcher* 1(1), 14–22.

Abbott, P. and Sapsford, R. (1992) *Research Methods for Nurses and the Caring Professions*. Buckingham: Open University Press.

Burnard, P. (1993) 'Facilities for searching the literature and storing references', *Nurse Researcher* 1(1), 56–63.

Clamp, C. G. L. (1994) *Resources for Nursing Research: An Annotated Bibliography*, 2nd edn. London: Library Association Publishing.

Gash, S. (1989) *Effective Literature Searching for Students*. Aldershot: Gower.

Gould, D. (1994) 'Writing literature reviews', *Nurse Researcher* 2(1), 13–23.

LoBiondo-Wood, G. and Haber, J. (eds) (1994) *Nursing Research: Methods, Critical Appraisal and Utilization*, 3rd edn. St Louis: The C.V. Mosby Co.

McSweeney, P. (1990) 'How to conduct a literature search', *Nursing* 4(3), 19–22.

Mason, C. (1993) 'Doing a research literature review', *Nurse Researcher* 1(1), 43–55.

Moorbath, P. (1993) 'The structure of the literature: varieties of journals and sources', *Nurse Researcher* 1(1), 4–13.

Polit, D. F., and Hungler, B. P. (1995) *Nursing Research: Principles and Methods*, 5th edn. Philadelphia: J. B. Lippincott Co.

Roddham, M. (1989) *Searching the Literature*, Research Awareness Module 4. London: Distance Learning Centre, South Bank University.

Roe, B. (1993) 'Undertaking a critical review of the literature', *Nurse Researcher* 1(1), 31–42.

CHAPTER 5
Approaches to and design of research in nursing

Learning outcomes

On completion of this chapter the reader should be able to
- identify the difference between inductive and deductive approaches to research.
- describe different approaches under the umbrella of inductive and deductive research.
- understand the main components of feminist research.
- appreciate the place of nursing practice in action research.

Key terms

deductive
ex post facto
experimental/quasi-experimental
inductive

qualitative
quantitative
survey

INTRODUCTION

There are many ways in which a researcher approaches the task of investigation. In the first instance a decision is made regarding the overall nature of the study – whether there is a theory to be tested (deductive research), or if it is purely investigatory in which it is perceived that a theory (or theories) will be developed (inductive).

Following on from that, the researcher may choose a theoretical framework which will guide and underpin the whole of the study. Within nursing this may be the use of a conceptual model of nursing, such as Roper, Logan and Tierney, to give focus and direction to the study. In the last 20 years nursing research has been using theories from other disciplines as a base. Traditionally, the medical model was followed and the biological sciences were used. Latterly, sociological theories, such as interactionism, have been used in an attempt to support the developing nursing ideals of a more holistic and individualized approach to care. Also borrowed from other sciences have been their perspectives, so that now nurse researchers may perform their research via a feminist or behaviourist position. Another element which may impinge on the researcher's approach to the study is the use of a philosophical framework such as phenomenology. This philosophy would appear to support the ideal of holistic nursing care and would lead the investigator to describe experiences (or phenomena) as they are lived (Oiler, 1982).

In designing a study the researcher has to consider the concept of time and location (Brink and Wood, 1978). In this chapter, various research designs such as prospective, retrospective, and *ex post facto* designs will be discussed. Sometimes research studies are categorized according to their location. The terms 'field' and 'laboratory' studies are frequently used and both have their advantages and disadvantages.

Before the researcher can begin the study, major decisions have to be made regarding the approach to be taken and the overall research design. The focus of the study will not be solely on the subject of the investigation but on the theory or the philosophical stance taken by the researcher.

The plethora of terms used to categorize different research studies will often confuse the newcomer to studying research. Quantitative research might be thought of as any type of research in which measurement is involved. The term quantitative may refer to both the method of collecting the data and the type of data involved. The criteria revolve around whether or not the data are already in the numerical form or can be easily transformed into numbers.

At their basic form, these numerical data will include the frequency with which a phenomenon occurs. At the more sophisticated end of the scale, exact measurements will be recorded under very strict conditions. The importance of recognizing the characteristics of these different levels of measurement will be emphasized and discussed fully in Chapter 9. The data collection methods most frequently employed in quantitative research include questionnaire, large-scale structured interviews, and experiments.

In order to produce data collecting tools or instruments which will accurately measure the phenomena being studied, the researcher will need to have considerable knowledge of the subject/phenomena under scrutiny. A frequent criticism of quantitative data is that there is not enough evidence that the data collecting tool is actually measuring the phenomena under study.

Researchers may not collect their own data but use those already collected by another agency. National archives hold data collected by various organizations both academic and governmental to which researchers may have access. Gilbert (1994) suggests that this type of research is gaining popularity among social researchers as it offers those with limited resources an opportunity to study large-scale data sets. With most hospitals now using computerized patient information systems of some kind, the amount of data which potentially could be available for nurse researchers is increasing all the time.

In contrast, qualitative research methods adopt a much more flexible approach to data collection. Observational studies in which behaviours are observed and fully recorded are rarely in numerical form. Similarly, focused interviews in which the researcher holds a conversation with the subjects produce data often described as 'rich' in their detail. Correspondingly, case studies involve a detailed investigation of an individual's life in all its aspects.

Thus, this one classification of research – qualitative and quantitative – identifies a design of research and, possibly more relevant, a type of data collection and therefore analysis. Although usually presented as fairly tight compartments, studies may include different methods of data collection which encompass both categories.

INDUCTIVE AND DEDUCTIVE APPROACHES TO RESEARCH

A further classification frequently seen in research texts is that of inductive and deductive/hypothetico-deductive research. It may be suggested that this classification gives a much wider understanding of the researcher's stance within the research study, which goes beyond simply the method of data collection.

Bassett (1994) cited Miller (1985) in his proposal that researchers need to consider various ideas prior to commencing a study. These ideas include the existing research based knowledge of the topic being studied, the purpose of the research (if the study is to discover information or to confirm existing knowledge), and the capability of the researcher to obtain the required data.

Possibly most important is the researcher's attitude to gaining knowledge. A major way in which new knowledge is gained is through logical reasoning and this falls into two categories: inductive and deductive reasoning. As research is about the gaining of new knowledge it makes sense that types of research are often identified under these two headings: inductive theory development and deductive theory testing.

It can be seen therefore that the inductive/deductive terminology is related to the place of theory within the study. In simplistic terms, inductive research generates theories which are then tested in deductive research.

Aggleton and Chalmers (1986) suggest that inductive and hypothetico-deductive approaches to research should be called methodologies. They argue that such approaches are more than a way of collecting data; they specify an overall commitment within a research process. From the literature it would appear that the other approaches to research, such as phenomenology and feminism, should also be referred to as methodologies as they identify a belief or position from which the researcher conducts the study.

INDUCTIVE APPROACHES

Inductive reasoning moves from the general to the particular. This approach in research encaptures the philosophy that people are fundamentally different from things and should be valued as individuals. As patterns of behaviour or interactions develop, the researcher seeks to make sense of them from the individual's perspective.

When undertaking inductive research there are several points that the researcher must be clear about regarding the approach to data collection. Initially, whatever data collection methods are used, a great effort must be made by the researcher not to influence the collection of data. This research approach demands that the picture painted is as close to the real situation as possible, as there is no attempt at interpretation. In the account of the observations, the physical environment is often described, as well as the speech and actions of individuals, so that a complete picture is painted.

From these ideas it may be seen that in undertaking inductive research a researcher may have certain beliefs about the individual in society. Talbot (1995) suggests that there should be a 'fit' between the research design and the researcher's philosophical orientation.

Under the umbrella of inductive research there are various approaches which require further discussion.

Ethnography

This approach has its roots in social anthropology when researchers lived among the group of individuals being studied. The term 'going native' has been coined from these early studies and from the work of ethnographers such as Mead in the 1930s who lived among tribes in Papua New Guinea (Haralambos, 1991). In more modern times 'going native' might refer to joining groups which are being studied such as a football supporters' club or a group of homeless individuals. Whatever group is being studied the crucial point is that of becoming an 'insider' and experiencing the group or organization 'as one of them', not as an outsider looking in. In her study of nursing culture and the place of ritual, Holland (1993) cites Spradley and Mann (1970) and uses their principles of observation on which to base her study. These principles include the belief that every culture creates its own reality, everyone takes their own culture for granted and that there is frequently more than one cultural perspective in any social situation. Holland (1993) identified a hospital ward as a cultural system which had its own economic system based around the working day, its own power distribution and a unique communication system with its own language.

In order to be able to study a group in such depth, the researcher has to enter the study without bias about the group or the questions to be asked. Through observations and in-depth questioning the researcher looks for connections, patterns and themes that have meaning for the people within that culture. These themes might include shared belief systems, language or role behaviours. To fulfil the role of ethnographer in its purest form the researcher should be a covert or hidden participant observer (see Chapter 8). This raises many ethical issues regarding who knows the true identity of the researcher, who 'owns' the data once they are collected and how issues of confidentiality are addressed.

Phenomenology

Phenomenology has its roots in European philosophy and is based on knowledge gained within the experiences of the individual and the individual's view of the world. In this approach the research question is explained through lived experiences as described by those being studied. There is a basic belief held by the researcher that individuals have attitudes, values and knowledge with which they make sense of their world and which guide their actions. Munhall and Oiler (1986; cited by Talbot, 1995) argue that the aim of phenomenology is to describe the experience being studied rather than attempt to define or explain it. Morse *et al.* (1994), in their investigation into patients' comfort, cite van Manen's (1990) description of the phenomenological process. In this there is an inter-relationship between exploring the lived experience and reflecting on the unique themes of the experience. Meanwhile, the researcher strives to capture the richness of the experience while maintaining a strong orientation to the fundamental research question (van Manen, 1990). By talking to patients who had suffered considerable pain, Morse *et al.* (1994) explored the term 'comfort' with their respondents and found that great difficulty was experienced in trying to put the idea of being comfortable into words. They concluded that the experience of comfort is more than the lack of discomfort, and the notion of mental comfort has to be added to that of physical comfort.

Grounded theory

Grounded theory as an approach to research was developed by Glaser and Strauss (1972). They generated a systematic procedure for developing a theory about a phenomenon from the collected data. As the researcher examines the data which have been collected by observations or interviews, themes and concepts are identified. The researcher then returns frequently to the data looking for further evidence of the themes and revising the research question as issues arise from the data. Hamill (1995) used a grounded theory approach in his study of stress in Diploma (Project 2000) students, as it allowed the respondents to articulate their own ideas about stress and permitted the researcher to be guided in his interviews by the data he was collecting.

To use grounded theory the researcher needs to have a background knowledge of the literature and people's experience of the situation being examined. The literature may be used to provide the researcher with prompts and guidance over the concepts related to the area under investigation. Talbot (1995) provides an interesting discussion of the use of literature in grounded theory. In many ways, grounded theory is perceived as the far end of the inductive continuum as theories are actually produced. In phenomenology and ethnography themes and categories describing behaviours in their social context are often left at that – the identification of themes and categories.

DEDUCTIVE APPROACHES

Deductive reasoning moves from the specific to the general. In research terms this means a prediction is made of the presence or not of a difference or a relationship between two or more factors (usually referred to as variables). The prediction is made through a hypothesis or measurable statement which can be deduced from a theory. This prediction will then be tested. The results of the research either will or will not support the prediction and confirm the deduction (or not).

In essence, deductive or hypothetico-deductive research depends on several considerations to withstand scrutiny. The first requirement is that of an existing theory on which to base the hypothesis and give the study a focus. Following that, a previously tested data collecting tool will be needed to collect information from a representative sample of the research population. The analysis of the results will demand rigorous statistical testing in which the possibility of these results occurring by chance will be demonstrated and discussed. Deductive research tends to be tightly managed and highly structured to allow the movement of the findings from the specific sample to a more general research population. This movement is sometimes referred to as the generalizability of the results.

Surveys

Surveys are widely used to collect information from a large number of people. They are primarily designed to study the relationship and incidence of variables such as attitudes and values and demographic details such as ages and types of living accommodation in a population. Questionnaires are frequently used to collect this information, with the respondent completing a self-administered form and returning it to the researcher. A telephone may also be used and the respondent's replies noted immediately. An example of a telephone survey is the study by Worth and Tierney (1993) in which they collected data from elderly people following their discharge from hospital. They found the method cost-effective but emphasized the need for an interview with the respondent prior to the telephone contact. The researcher has to acknowledge that a number of people will just put the telephone down and those who have particular hearing difficulties may need to be excluded from the sample (as do those without a telephone). Also in surveys, face-to-face interviews are used in which the researcher tends to obtain more information and a high rate of returns (few people refuse to be interviewed), but it is a time-consuming procedure and the sample would be much smaller than that when a questionnaire is used.

Two main examples of surveys are sample surveys such as the large-scale public opinion studies like Gallup Polls, in which a sample of people are asked their opinions, and the census completed every ten years, in which everyone in the country is questioned. Most surveys documented in the literature are sample surveys.

Experimental/quasi-experimental designs in research

In the research discussed thus far the researcher has been a collector of data, a passive observer (Polit and Hungler, 1993). In experimental research, the researcher is interested in the effect of different treatments on two or more groups which have been matched in every other way. Usually this means manipulating the independent variable (or cause) and examining and measuring the dependent variable (or effect).

In true experimental research the investigator is an active agent who has responsibility in three specific areas.

(a) *Randomization* – subjects are assigned to the experimental or control group in a randomized manner. Everyone in the study must have an equal chance of being included in either group.
(b) *Control* – there must be a control group who receive the traditional or usual care/treatment.
(c) *Manipulation* – the researcher must have an experimental group receiving different care/treatment.

When these three conditions are stringently applied, the results of true experiments in examining a causal relationship are most powerful.

Although the results of experiments are powerful, there are many problems using them. The ethical considerations associated with using human beings in experiments limit their use. Polit and

Hungler (1993) also suggest that a problem with using experiments is that of the 'Hawthorne effect', in which people alter their behaviour when they know they are part of a study. When this happens the results of the experiment might be affected.

Because of these problems in conducting experiments, the notion of quasi-experiments has been developed. In this there is still the manipulation of the independent variable, but there may be limited randomization or use of a control group. The results of quasi-experiments are therefore considerably weaker than those of true experiments. The term quasi-experiment is also used to describe experimental studies which lack one or more of the conditions noted above.

In the most controlled settings a laboratory is used. It does not have to look like a traditional laboratory, as buildings have been made to look like prisons or hospital wards to set up an experiment. Yet they are still laboratory experiments.

The alternative is to use a field approach. In this type of experiment the research is conducted wherever the subjects are likely to be found, such as in a clinic, a hospital ward or in the street. Often field experiments are quasi-experiments as it is so difficult to control all variables. Experiments which take place in clinical settings involving patients/clients are commonly called randomized controlled trials (RCT).

Ex post facto research designs

Ex post facto literally means 'after the fact'. In these studies there is an investigation about a relationship between two or more variables, but after things have been allowed to happen in the natural course of events.

The two most common forms of *ex post facto* research designs are retrospective and prospective studies. In retrospective studies the researcher will want to study an effect and will search for some causative factor of that effect. Prospective studies are conducted in the light of presumed causes. Researchers will follow their subjects forward in time and look for the effect of the causes. Prospective studies are usually expensive and time-consuming because of the need to follow up subjects, but they do allow the researcher a greater degree of control.

Feminist research

From its beginnings as research conducted by feminists, feminist research has developed into a research methodology in its own right. Webb (1993) cites Cormack (1981) in her definition of feminist research as involving 'a set of principles of inquiry: a feminist philosophy of science', and adds that feminist research is carried out *for* women. Feminist research attempts to redress the balance of many years of male dominance in explanations of what happens in our society. It does this by developing a non-threatening, non-hierarchical relationship between the researcher and the subjects, and by making women the focus of the study.

There is some argument regarding the position of men conducting feminist research. In principle some believe it possible (Harding, 1987; cited in Webb, 1993); others believe that men, by not encountering a woman's experience, are unable to conduct the research from a woman's position (Kremer, 1990; cited in Webb, 1993). As an added element to the discussion of men's place in feminist research Webb (1993) cites Wise (1987) who proposes that as feminist research often centres on women's oppression and as this oppression is by men, men should be included in feminist research. In an attempt to recognize exactly what is feminist research Cook and Fonow (1986) identified five characteristics:

(a) the attention given to the significance of gender
(b) consciousness-raising (of women's issues)
(c) a rejection of the concept of objectivity
(d) the recognition of the exploitation of women
(e) the empowerment of women as a result of the research.

As a methodology feminist research is not constrained by a particular data collecting method. However, the very nature of feminist research, in which there is involvement of the researcher with the researched and a sharing of experiences, would imply a need for a more open inductive research approach rather than a closed deductive approach.

Action research

Action research is an approach which attempts to bring about an immediate change in practice. This occurs through action and reflection on that action while developing an improvement in practice. Thus action research may be described as a spiral of self-reflection in which individuals question the familiar and explore the unfamiliar (Stark, 1994). Alongside the change in practice is the development and testing of theories using hypotheses. According to Titchen and Binnie (1994) there are two main elements: outsider and insider research. The insiders refer to the practitioners who are developing their practice while being involved in the research. The outsider is the researcher who observes the insider's practice and provides an opportunity for the insider to rationalize and discuss the practice, while examining the methodological considerations. Titchen and Binnie (1994) used their developing double act of insider and outsider to examine the move from traditional nursing to a patient-centred organization of care. The research was conducted with the researchers being immersed in the setting in which the research took place.

Action research attempts to influence the real world of practice by identifying changes as they take place rather than generating theories. However, there is an argument that action research should begin by observations either completed in a prior study or as a preliminary of the action research in which theories may have been generated.

In an attempt to locate action research, Titchen and Binnie (1994) propose that, like experiments, there is the active involvement of the researcher. Action research is dependent on the researcher/ practitioner changing practice while the research is in progress, much like the way the experimenter would manipulate the variables. However, unlike experiments, there is no attempt to generalize the results of action research through statistical testing and probability theory. The results of action research are analysed as inductive research, in which a situation is described, interpreted and explanations attempted.

In her discussion of action research, Meyer (1993) acknowledges that action research might be seen as a way in which research is made more accessible to practising nurses. With the great interest in the work of Schon (1991) and 'reflection-in-action', it might be suggested that action research is a more systematic way of using the principles of reflection to improve the practice of those conducting the research and allow the research/practitioners to act as role models for other nurses.

In some research papers, it might be noted that the term 'triangulation' occurs. This is an idea taken from the world of surveyors, when, to locate a point, measurements are taken from different positions. In research, triangulation is used to measure the same problem or concept using different data collecting methods or approaches. The idea is that the results are strengthened if the researcher uses different research methods and arrives at similar conclusions.

Key points

- The place of theory within the research is important.
- Inductive research attempts to develop a theory.
- Deductive research tests theories.
- Both these categories have further sub-divisions.
- Action research attempts to change practice while the research is ongoing.
- Feminist research has its own agenda and is not tied to a specific data collecting method.

FURTHER READING

Cushing, A. (1994) 'Historical and epistemological perspectives on research and nursing', *Journal of Advanced Nursing* 20(3), 406–11.
Greenwood, J. (1994) 'Action research: a few details, a caution and something new', *Journal of Advanced Nursing* 20(1), 13–18.
Hakim, C. (1987) *Research Design*. London: Unwin.
Martin, P. (1995) 'Qualitative nursing research: the issues and pitfalls', *Nursing Times* 91(12), 44–5.
Meyer, J. (1993) 'New paradigm research in practice: the trials and tribulations of action research', *Journal of Advanced Nursing* 18(7), 1066–72.
Morse, J. (ed.) (1991) *Qualitative Nursing Research*. London: Sage.
Siebold, C., Richards, L. and Simon, D. (1994) 'Feminist method and qualitative research about midlife', *Journal of Advanced Nursing* 19(2), 394–402.
Webb, C. (1993) 'Feminist research: definitions, methodology, methods and evaluation', *Journal of Advanced Nursing* 18(3), 416–23.

CHAPTER 6
Research aims, questions and hypotheses

Learning outcomes

On completion of this chapter the reader should be able to
- appreciate the nature of research problems.
- understand the formation of research questions.
- recognize the difference between research questions and hypotheses.
- identify independent and dependent variables.

Key terms

dependent variable   null hypothesis
hypothesis   research problem
independent variable   research question

INTRODUCTION

Nursing is a 'practice based' profession, and it therefore follows that practice should influence the identification of problems and questions that are researchable. These 'problems' may have their foundation in the experience of nurses and nursing, or they may come from the literature, or they may emerge from an existing theory. When considering clinical nursing research, McGowan (1994; cited in Robertson, 1994) suggests that a researchable problem could be one where the current method of addressing the problem is unsatisfactory to the nurses or patients. She also suggests that proposed solutions to problems should improve patient care, and that nurses should be able to implement any proposed changes.

Researchable problems could also come from the results of previous research that has identified some new problems.

In many instances, a problem in practice is identified locally by a nurse who feels that something is 'not quite right'. However, the nurse may not be in any position to do something about the problem. The Briggs Report (Department of Health and Social Security, 1972) recommended that 'direct research into clinical nursing and midwifery problems ... should begin in the ward itself or at field level in the community' (para. 374). This implies that nurses in clinical practice need to be able to identify problems that are researchable. More recently, *The Report of the Taskforce on the Strategy for Research in Nursing, Midwifery and Health Visiting* (Department of Health, 1993b) made this more explicit and stated: 'Nurses, Health Visitors and Midwives need an understanding of the research process, the ability to retrieve and critically assess research findings and literature, and through those skills, the ability to help define research problems, agenda and priority' (p. 13, para. 3.3.2).

Other chapters have considered the skills needed by nurses to retrieve and critically evaluate research findings and literature, and Chapter 3 deliberates upon the research process. This chapter examines research questions, aims and hypotheses, and takes up the position that nursing research questions often arise from problems in practice. In addition, the priorities for research may emerge from problems rooted in practice. Nurses need to understand and identify research problems, which can then form the basis of a researchable question. They may not necessarily be involved in undertaking the research. However, they have an important role in identifying researchable questions and setting the agenda for research in clinical practice.

Research problems may also be generated by large organizations who, in turn, identify priorities for research. These priorities will be clearly distinguished, and funding awarded for appropriate studies that address the problems. The Department of Health is currently funding research into cancers and mental health problems, as well as other priorities within the health services.

At an early stage in the research process, a researcher needs to refine the problem into clear researchable questions. The way in which a research question is interpreted, however, is dependent on the beliefs, values, experience and approach of the researcher. When reading research, nurses should always be aware of the researcher's influence in the way that research questions have been interpreted from the research problem.

As identified in Chapter 5, there are two broad approaches in research – deductive and inductive. A deductive approach will use primarily quantitative methods of data collection and analysis to test a theory. On the basis of a theory, and prior to data collection, researchers will make predictions about what will happen in specific situations. An inductive approach, however, will use mainly qualitative methods of data collection and analysis with the aim of examining the data for patterns and relationships. The purpose is to understand and describe what is going on, with a view to generating a theory. Predictions may be generated from the data and tested and retested during the course of the research. However, research using this approach will not usually begin with a prediction about what will be found.

RESEARCH AIMS AND OBJECTIVES

Many researchers will identify aims and objectives at the beginning of their study. These will guide the researcher and give some indication of what the researcher is trying to achieve. Aims and objectives are not particularly specific; indeed, they may be intentionally vague. They may identify the purpose of the research, and they may suggest goals or outcomes in quite general terms. However, they do not give a clear indication of what questions are being asked, and they do not give any prediction as to what they are expecting to find. Both qualitative and quantitative studies may incorporate research aims and objectives.

RESEARCH QUESTIONS

In order to be able to manage a research project, the details of the study need to be made much more explicit, and this is often made clear through the research question(s). Some studies will have more than one research question, or there may be a principal question, followed by a few questions that are more specific. If there is more than one question, they must be clearly related. Most research will have research questions posed at the outset of the study, and qualitative studies using an inductive approach will continue to be guided by the questions. Exploratory studies, in particular, will identify research questions, occasionally with a view to generating and testing a theory from the descriptive findings of the study.

Clearly articulating and defining the research question is often identified as one of the most difficult stages in the research process. Cormack and Benton (Cormack, 1991, p. 67) suggest that a 'good' research question 'clearly states or implies a relationship between two or more variables'. The variables stated must be capable of observation and measurement. A research question can either be a statement in question form, or a statement of a purpose: 'What is the relationship between the provision of post-registration education and the retention of staff?', or 'The purpose of this study is to investigate the relationship between the provision of post-registration education and the retention of staff' (Cormack and Benton, 1991; cited in Cormack, 1991, p. 67).

When reading research reports, nurses need to be able to identify the source of the research question, and how it has been developed from the problem. In some reports, only the problem is identified through a problem statement. If this is the case, the problem needs clearly to identify and define the research variables and the nature of the population being studied. In other types of research, neither the problem nor the research questions will be identified. However, there should be a specific purpose to the study which identifies why the study is being conducted.

RESEARCH HYPOTHESES

In some approaches to research, a hypothesis is devised before the study begins and will guide the whole study. The hypothesis goes further than a research question and is directly related to the research problem. It is used primarily, although not exclusively, in quantitative studies using a deductive approach. The hypothesis is a statement about the relationship between two or more variables and predicts an expected outcome. Variables are any characteristics about a person that can vary: age, sex, height, eye colour etc. In some studies, the variables need to be clearly defined because they are not always obvious. The hypothesis will also determine who and what is to be studied, and the way that the findings are interpreted.

Unlike a research question, a hypothesis will predict what will happen in a particular study and it can be a very powerful and persuasive tool. Locke *et al.* (1993, p. 15) explain the differences between research questions and hypotheses very clearly:

At the end of a study, a research question never permits the investigator to say more than 'this is how the world looked when I observed it'. In contrast, hypotheses permit the investigator to say, 'based on my particular explanation about how the world works, this is what I expected to observe, and behold – that is exactly how it looked! For that reason my explanation of how the world works must be given credibility'. When a hypothesis is confirmed, the investigator is empowered to make arguments about knowledge that go far beyond what is available when a question has been asked and answered. (Locke *et al.*, 1993, p. 15)

Table 6.1   Independent and dependent variables within hypotheses

Older nurses are less likely to express positive comments about the extended role of the nurse than younger nurses.
* Age of nurse is the independent variable.
* Positive comments about the extended role of the nurse is the dependent variable.

Patients who receive a copy of the 'Patient's Charter' ask more questions about their care than those who do not receive it.
* Receiving/not receiving the 'Patient's Charter' is the independent variable.
* Number of questions asked is the dependent variable.

Absenteeism is higher in Mental Health Branch students than Child Branch students.
* Type of Branch student is the independent variable.
* Number of days absent is the dependent variable.

Elderly patients in residential care who experience back massage express greater satisfaction of nursing care than those who do not receive back massage.
* Back massage is the independent variable.
* Satisfaction with nursing care is the dependent variable.

A hypothesis should be clear, concise, logical and specific enough for a reader to understand what the variables are and who the researcher will be studying. A hypothesis will predict a relationship between variables (e.g., difference, greater than, less than, positively, negatively, etc.) and, through testing, may or may not allow the relationship to be supported. There are two types of variable – independent variables and dependent variables. The independent variable is the 'treatment' or 'intervention' variable in the predicted relationship stated in the hypothesis; and the dependent variable is the 'outcome' variable in the relationship. This is commonly known as the 'cause and effect' relationship. There are some examples in Table 6.1.

A hypothesis can also be stated as a 'null' hypothesis. The null hypothesis states that there is *no* relationship between the variables. The null hypothesis is the preferred approach in some quantitative studies and is associated with tests of statistical significance. Hypotheses and null hypotheses are never 'proved' or 'disproved' in the truest sense of the word. They are accepted or rejected.

All nurses need to be able to recognize research aims, questions and hypotheses when they are reading research reports. The research questions or hypotheses identified should be clearly linked with the original research problem. Not all studies will have a hypothesis. However, where there is one, it should be clearly stated with at least two variables.

Key points

- Researchable problems have their foundations in practice, literature or an existing theory.
- An early stage in the research process is the identification of research aims, questions and hypotheses which must relate to the problem.
- A hypothesis is a statement about a relationship between two or more variables and predicts an expected outcome.

FURTHER READING

Buckeldee, J. and McMahon, R. (eds) (1994) *The Research Process in Nursing*. London: Chapman & Hall.

Burgess, R. G. (ed.) (1986) *Key Variables in Social Investigation*. London: Routledge and Kegan Paul.

Herbert, M. (1990) *Planning a Research Project*. London: Cassell.

LoBiondo-Wood, G. and Haber, J. (eds) (1994) *Nursing Research: Methods, Critical Appraisal, and Utilization*, 3rd edn. St Louis: Mosby.

Locke, L. F., Spirduso, W. W. and Silverman, S. J. (1993) *Proposals That Work*, 3rd edn. London: Sage.

Marshall, C. and Rossman, G. B. (1995) *Designing Qualitative Research*, 2nd edn. London: Sage.

Polit, D. and Hungler, B. (1995) *Nursing Research: Principles and Methods*, 5th edn. Philadelphia: J. B. Lippincott Co.

Robertson, J. (ed.) (1994) *Clinical Nursing Research*. London: Churchill Livingstone.

CHAPTER 7
Sampling

Learning outcomes

On completion of the chapter the reader should be able to
- understand definitions of research populations and samples.
- identify different sampling strategies that can be employed to select probability and non-probability samples.
- consider issues surrounding gaining access to populations and samples.
- appreciate the factors that affect sample selection, including sampling criteria and sample size.

Key terms

bias
cluster sample
convenience/accidental sample
generalization
non-probability sample
probability sample
purposive sample
quota sample
representative sample

sample
sampling
selection criteria
simple random sample
snowball sample
stratified sample
systematic sample
target population

INTRODUCTION

Sampling is used in everyday life, for example, when we taste a sip of wine before selecting to purchase a bottle or case of it; or at the grocers we might handle and smell fruit before purchase. Sampling involves the collection of information on which decisions can be based and conclusions drawn. If we liked the taste of the sampled wine we expect to get the same pleasure from bottles containing the same vintage, but could not be certain of our reactions if we purchased a vintage which we had not sampled.

Researchers must collect information from chosen samples, which is then used to make decisions and draw conclusions, just as the purchaser of wine. The selection of the sample is therefore a very important part of the research process. The researcher needs to be confident in drawing conclusions based on the information collected from the chosen sample. Errors in sampling have the potential to invalidate the research findings and render the research unusable.

Before a sample is selected the researcher identifies a target population, using techniques which fall into two main sampling strategies: probability and non-probability sampling. Prior to describing these strategies, the terms target population and sample must be understood.

TARGET POPULATION

The target population includes the entire membership of the group in which the researcher is interested and from which information can be collected. Such populations might include all student nurses following Diploma of Higher Education in Nursing Studies (DipHE NS, Project 2000) courses, all National Health Service (NHS) Trust Hospitals, all E Grade Staff Nurses. Researchers may also collect information from clinical situations or documents, and in these cases the target population may include all cardio-pulmonary resuscitation attempts, or all completed nursing care plans.

The researcher can assign eligibility criteria to the target population, defining limits within which the target population must fall. For example, the researcher may be interested in the students following the Adult Branch of the Diploma (Project 2000) course rather than those following the Mental Health, Child and Learning Disabilities Branches. It is therefore necessary to define the target population as students following the Adult Branch of the Diploma (Project 2000) course and select a sample of students who meet this criterion.

The definition of criteria by the researcher facilitates the generalization (application) of the research findings. In the example given above, research findings could only reliably be applied to students following the Diploma (Project 2000) course, Adult Branch. The degree to which results can be generalized is referred to as external validity. External validity can be an important factor in research. However, it should be acknowledged that not all researchers are interested in achieving external validity. Researchers using an inductive approach (see Chapter 5) will value the quality of the information collected rather than the ability to generalize the findings to a larger population.

SAMPLING

It is unlikely that the researcher will be able to collect information from the entire target population. This would be both time-consuming and expensive. The researcher collects information from a representative sample of the target population, selected by taking a sample from the target population.

A sample is a portion or part of the target population, composed of members (elements or subjects) from which information is collected. In nursing research, the target population may be a patient or client group and the sample will be a portion of that patient or client group.

The most important feature of sampling is the degree to which the sample represents the target population. For the sample to be representative, the members need to reflect the constitution of the target population in as many ways as possible. For example, how closely do the characteristics or variables such as gender, age, medical diagnosis of the sample, reflect those of the target population?

The reduction of sampling bias is also of importance and can be seen if one part of the target population is over-represented or under-represented in the sample. For example, if the researcher was interested in measuring the effectiveness of health promotion strategies and chose to sample people attending health promotion clinics, it could be argued that those attending the clinics could have strong views about the benefits of the clinics, so could be a biased sample.

Limiting the difference between the target population and the sample is achieved to varying degrees through the application of accepted sampling techniques in the selection of samples. The two strategies used to select a sample are probability and non-probability sampling.

PROBABILITY SAMPLES

Probability sampling involves the use of random selection in obtaining the sample members. The use of random selection allows the researcher to state the probability of a member of the target population appearing in the sample. In some cases all members of the target population may have an equal chance of appearing in the sample. Probability sampling limits sampling errors and bias, increases sample representativeness and gives confidence in the sample. It is therefore the preferred sampling strategy when the researcher is interested in obtaining a representative sample.

Simple random sample

In generating a simple random sample the basic technique of probability sampling is used. When the entire population is known, the use of simple random sampling gives each member of the target population an equal chance of being included in the sample. This occurs through the design of a sampling frame in which all members of the target population are represented and from which the sample will be chosen. For example, Moule (1992, unpublished dissertation) selected a target population of Diploma (Project 2000) course students located at a college in the south-west of England. The list of all Diploma (Project 2000) students at the college formed the sampling frame. Thus, every student at the college had an equal chance of selection.

In this example the sampling frame was generated by the researcher, but in some research an existing sampling frame may be used. If a researcher was interested in sampling qualified and practising nurses, midwives and health visitors, then the Register held by the United Kingdom Central Council for Nurses, Midwives and Health Visitors could be accessed and used as a sampling frame.

The use of existing sampling frames can be effective in accessing a sample but a sampling frame needs to be selected appropriately, to avoid introducing sampling bias. For example, the telephone directory is used by many market researchers as a sampling frame. However, it should be acknowledged that as a sampling frame the telephone directory will be an incomplete list of the residents of a community. Not every resident will have a telephone and those with a telephone could be ex-directory. The telephone directory will not offer a complete sampling frame and will not therefore facilitate probability sampling.

Table 7.1 Random number table

03	35	11	98	74	20	23	61	32	30
07	09	15	22	21	88	94	90	50	71
84	10	02	91	24	35	47	63	99	04
13	82	31	44	70	65	38	80	92	01
23	33	18	76	97	06	64	53	70	98
17	21	09	05	14	30	31	82	54	56
77	62	02	19	27	48	59	92	71	25
66	04	12	55	42	60	83	24	37	22
05	90	08	69	33	93	57	74	29	10
30	44	74	28	09	67	24	18	99	81
45	89	12	75	65	22	48	21	08	55
78	26	72	03	28	91	36	42	10	89
88	56	23	14	73	54	22	07	52	39
25	78	65	91	63	45	71	01	86	49
67	04	30	05	73	29	96	39	24	49
14	71	27	18	46	28	34	97	24	12
16	48	73	92	45	29	37	19	28	10
13	85	49	37	40	16	72	95	41	08
17	39	73	37	19	91	65	28	76	95
45	42	97	28	02	36	73	95	46	99
77	54	28	16	34	07	16	94	73	54
65	48	27	04	62	48	37	19	21	45
24	91	54	38	18	35	42	87	06	72
06	12	21	26	29	44	79	13	19	46
12	05	43	05	51	10	78	36	58	25
18	25	37	19	54	28	75	53	24	82
96	14	52	75	62	01	99	53	24	42
45	68	24	02	15	73	57	28	27	25
56	81	72	24	04	38	26	78	15	29

Having generated or obtained an existing sampling frame, the researcher proceeds to select sufficient members randomly from the frame to meet the sample size needed for the study. This can be achieved through the use of a random number table (see Table 7.1) or more inventive methods such as selecting names from a hat or using a blindfold and a pin. The use of the random number table necessitates numbering the sampling frame members and then selecting, from the sampling frame, the numbers which correspond to those on the random number table. If selecting a sample of ten from the random number table in Table 7.1, the following numbered members would be included in the sample: 03, 35, 11, 98, 74, 20, 23, 61, 32, 30.

In selecting a simple random sample it is apparent that the researcher cannot intentionally introduce sampling bias. Any bias which may occur will do so by accident, as a result of chance. The likelihood of introducing bias by chance will reduce as the size of the sample selected increases.

It is also apparent that the use of simple random sampling is laborious, and, despite the availability of computer software to generate random numbers, is time-consuming. Simple random sampling is used infrequently in sample selection when a sampling frame is available. The technique of random selection is also seen in other probability sampling strategies.

Systematic random sample

In selecting a systematic random sample a similar technique to that of simple random sampling is employed, as a list of the target population is used to form a sampling frame from which the sample is selected on a systematic basis. In selecting systematically, the researcher may select, for example, every tenth member on the list or every hundredth member. In this way, all members have an equal chance of being selected into the population, provided that all members of the target population are included in the sampling frame.

It is possible to select the sample by first calculating the sampling interval for a target population (interval needed between each target member to be selected). To calculate the sampling interval, the researcher would need to know the total number in the target population and the sample size required. For example, if the total target population were 2000 patients who attended an outpatients department, and the sample size required were 100 (2000/100 = 20), then the sample interval is 20. The researcher would select every twentieth patient, following on from the first patient selected from the sampling frame. If the first patient selected was identified as number 2, then patients 22, 42, 62, 82, 102 etc. would form the sample.

This sampling technique was applied by Hinojosa (1992) to select 40 hospital records of patients who were admitted for a cholecystectomy in one hospital between April 1986 and April 1988. A computer list of the hospital records was printed by the Medical Records Department, which met eligibility criteria set and included all completed and uncomplicated cholecystectomy procedures. The sampling frame was therefore composed of all hospital records of patients having uncomplicated cholecystectomy surgery between

April 1986 and April 1988. Using a sampling frame, the researcher selected every third hospital record, to achieve a sample size of 40 ($n = 40$).

Systematic sampling offers a more efficient way of selecting a random sample, and the only way that bias can be introduced is by chance. For example, if every third patient selected by Hinojosa (1992) possessed a particular characteristic, that characteristic would be over-represented in the sample. In this example, every third patient may be a diabetic patient, or may have been female, or of a particular ethnic group. A sample thus composed could be argued to be biased and interpretation of the research findings would need to acknowledge this. As with simple random sampling, the chance of bias would be reduced as the size of the sample increased.

Stratified random sample

Selecting a stratified random sample involves the subdivision of the target population into strata, before developing a sampling frame from which a random sample is selected. It is dependent upon the researcher having knowledge of the characteristics or variables of the population, which are important to achieving a representative sample. Subdivision could relate to any variable or characteristic of the target population, such as age, sex, height, weight, ethnic group, socio-economic status, delivery of specified nursing care, diagnosis, period of admission to hospital, drug prescriptions etc.

Selecting a sample in this way can help achieve a representative sample with a smaller sample size, so can facilitate more effective use of resources, especially time and money. For example, if a researcher was collecting opinions from Registered General Nurses (RGN) about sexual harassment at work, it would be important for the sample to represent the percentage of male and female RGNs in the workforce. If the proportion of male RGNs were 10 per cent and female RGNs were 90 per cent, then a proportionate sample would reflect this.

In some instances the researcher may feel it important to have equal numbers of respondents in the sample to obtain a more balanced view, in this case 50 per cent male and 50 per cent female RGNs. This would be a disproportionate sample, as it does not represent the male and female composition of the RGN group. The researcher would need to adjust the analysis of any results to compensate for this, by weighting responses. Explanation of this procedure is beyond the scope of this introductory text, but can be found in Kidder and Judd (1987, cited as further reading below, p. 74).

Stratified random sampling was used by Pruitt (1992) in evaluating the effect of a stress management programme as a component of a fitness programme. The sample was drawn from US army employees, 64 in total, who were stratified according to a measure of their life stressors, obtained using a Life Experiences Survey (Sarason *et al.*, 1985; cited in Pruitt, 1992). Following stratification, the sample was randomly assigned to either a control or an experimental group (see Chapter 5 for an explanation of experimental design).

Stratified sampling enables the researcher to use a smaller sample size to obtain the same measure of representation achieved from a larger simple random sample. It is therefore more time- and cost-effective for the researcher, as using a smaller sample size reduces time spent on data collection and analysis. Sampling error is decreased, as variables within the target population which are critical to the research are represented through stratification. To achieve this, the researcher has to have knowledge of the target population and therefore more effort is required in selecting a sample this way. For example, Pruitt (1992) needed to measure the life stressors of the sample to stratify the sample on this basis.

Cluster sample

Selecting a cluster sample is a more efficient way of accessing a larger sample than through simple or stratified sampling, and is often used to select samples for large-scale surveys, particularly in large geographical areas. Cluster samples can be obtained in situations where a sampling frame cannot be developed using individual members of the target population, as members are not all known to the researcher. This may occur if, for example, the target population were all patients having recovered from surgery.

Cluster sampling can also be referred to as multi-stage sampling, as the researcher selects the sample by following through a number of stages. For example, if the researcher wanted to access surgical patients, a sampling frame composed of organizations treating surgical patients would be developed and used to select patients randomly as sample members. The sampling frame may include Regional Health Authorities, hospitals, units, wards and, finally, patients admitted to the wards. The researcher would first select a Regional Health Authority and then randomly select hospitals within that Regional Health Authority. Surgical units would then be selected from the hospitals, and surgical wards within those units would form the penultimate sample, with patients on the wards being the final sampling frame.

Cluster sampling is more prone to sampling error than simple, stratified and systematic sampling, but offers the researcher a more efficient way of sampling when a large-scale survey is required. As shown in the example, the technique can also be valuable to the researcher who does not have a sampling frame composed of individual target population members, but is able to commence the sampling process with a sampling frame of organizations or institutions. By following multistage sampling techniques, the required sample will be accessed.

NON-PROBABILITY SAMPLES

Non-probability sampling techniques do not use random selection to gather together the sample. Researchers using non-probability sampling will not be able to state the probability of target population members being selected in the sample, as not every member of the target population has a chance of being selected in the sample. Non-probability sampling is more convenient to use, cost-effective and can be used to select a research sample when the researcher does not know the membership of the target population. Non-probability sampling techniques include convenience (accidental) sampling, quota sampling, purposive (judgemental) sampling and snowball (network) sampling.

Convenience (accidental) sample

When employing convenience or accidental sampling techniques the researcher obtains sufficient participants from the local or convenient target population. Participants are included in the sample because they are accessible. For example, a researcher considering the management of patients' post-operative pain may select a sample of post-operative patients from a local surgical ward, rather than travelling some distance to obtain a sample.

This is an uncomplicated approach to sampling, which is time- and cost-effective. Consequently, convenience sampling is a commonly used method. Ellis (1995) describes the use of convenience sampling when conducting a pilot study which considered the feasibility of providing patients in the community with timed visits from district nurses. The pilot study was conducted in Oldham NHS Trust, using a sample of district nurses from the same Trust.

When employing convenience sampling techniques, it is important for the researcher to acknowledge any limitations in the sample. Convenience sampling is the weakest sampling technique because bias may be introduced into the sample, which is difficult to identify and therefore any effect on the results can be difficult to judge. Bias can result from the over-representation or under-representation of portions of the target population, or from the effect of the researcher sampling locally from a population that is known. Bias may also result if the participants self-select themselves into the sample, through perhaps responding to market researchers in the street or to advertisements for research participants.

Quota sample

Selecting a quota sample involves the application of principles which are similar to those used to select a stratified random sample. The researcher uses knowledge of the target population to ensure that certain variables or characteristics of the target population are represented in the sample. The researcher may wish to include any number of variables in the sample, to represent males and females, socio-economic groups, patients with certain nursing needs, presence of disease or certain behaviour. By ensuring certain variables are represented in the sample, quota sampling offers a more reliable sampling technique than convenience sampling, as it attempts to limit some potential biases.

Royayne *et al.* (1989) used a quota sample when examining the differences in beliefs and social influences between patients with chronic peripheral vascular disease, who decided to either stop or continue smoking. The sample were English speaking and had a confirmed diagnosis of chronic peripheral vascular disease, which necessitated them attending a vascular clinic at a large teaching hospital. The sample were obtained from the clinic, through a process of quota sampling, with 20 who had stopped smoking and 22 who had continued smoking forming the sample. Given the area of research, it was important to have representation from patients who were diagnosed as having chronic peripheral vascular disease, and to have representation of smokers and those who had stopped smoking, which was achieved through quota sampling.

Purposive (judgemental) sample

A purposive sample is selected using the researcher's judgement, with no external objective method being used in sample selection. Reliance on the researcher could be inappropriate and lead to the selection of a biased sample. For example, the researcher may choose sample members who will reflect a certain viewpoint.

Purposive sampling can be a useful sampling technique to employ when the researcher wants to obtain a particular sample which cannot easily be selected through any other technique. For example, Hardy (1982) used purposive sampling to research the career histories of some leading female nurses in England and Scotland. Hardy (1982) purposefully chose 223 positional nurse leaders in England and Scotland, using the *Hospitals and Health Services Year Book* (1981; cited in Hardy, 1982) and *The Directory of Schools of Nursing* (1980; cited in Hardy, 1982). This group then became the purposive sample. This sampling technique enabled Hardy (1982) to gain access to a sample of influential nurses, who could not have been selected using other sampling techniques.

Snowball (network) sample

A snowball sample, sometimes referred to as a network sample, can be a useful technique for selecting a 'hidden' sample group, such as the homeless. Snowball sampling is based on the assumption that people with like characteristics, behaviours or interests form associations, and it is this relationship which the researcher uses to select a sample. For example, access to a group of experts can be gained by approaching one expert who recommends possible further respondents. Access to AIDS sufferers, the homeless, drug abusers, alcoholics can be obtained through one group member, who recommends further sample members and thus a self-generating sample is facilitated. Biases can be introduced as the sample is not independently selected and the sample could perpetuate particular traits. However, it can be a useful way of selecting a sample from marginalized groups.

To access a sample of people with AIDS, Nolan (1994; cited in Buckeldee and McMahon, 1994) used snowball sampling. Nolan approached health care workers engaged in therapeutic and helping relationships with people with AIDS, who then selected the research sample. The same technique was employed by Buenting (1992), who distributed questionnaires through women's book stores, community groups and gay and lesbian organizations to obtain a sample of heterosexual and lesbian women.

ISSUES RELATING TO SAMPLE SIZE

The selection of the sample, using the techniques described in the chapter, is as important as the size of the sample. A technique known as power analysis can be applied to estimate an appropriate sample size. This can be applied particularly in quantitative studies, when statistical tests are applied to the results and when the generalization of results to a wider population is of importance. The discussion of power analysis is beyond the scope of this introductory text, but can be found in Burns and Grove (1993; included as further reading below, p. 74).

It is generally accepted that a larger probability sample will give greater accuracy to the results, as the effect of over-representation or under-representation is reduced as the sample size increases. Non-probability samples may use a smaller sample size more effectively, particularly if the researcher is concerned with the quality of the information collected (qualitative approach), rather than the quantity of information which could be gathered (quantitative approach). Whichever sampling technique is used, it is the representative nature of the sample that is of greater importance than the size.

GAINING ACCESS TO SUBJECTS

In order to undertake research, and obviously prior to selecting a sample, it is necessary to gain access to the sources of data. In nursing research these are generally people, but could also be records or documents. Sometimes the sources of the data will be 'protected' and the researcher may need to negotiate carefully with people in powerful positions, or with institutions. The term 'gatekeeper' is often used to describe people who are attempting to safeguard the interests of others. These could, for example, be teachers protecting their students, or clinical managers protecting ward staff. Some researchers may offer something in return for giving access, such as a report. When research is taking place in a clinical setting, such as a ward or health centre, the researcher will need to gain permission from key individuals such as clinical managers. If patients are involved, the proposed research will need to be considered by a local Research Ethics Committee (see Chapter 10).

Acquiring permission or consent of the subjects is also an important factor in gaining access. This can be particularly difficult when the research is covert, such as participant observational studies.

Many ethical issues will need to be considered by the researcher, such as deception, concealment and not gaining consent from subjects who will clearly need to be protected. Berg (1989) discusses the importance of having the 'right attitude' when trying to negotiate access. Berg (1989) also suggests that researchers need to take a neutral position which allows them to understand what is going on, rather than appearing as either advocates or critics. Dealing with gatekeepers and negotiating access is a responsibility that all researchers must take seriously in order to protect research integrity. When reading research critically, nurses must consider the ways that the researcher may have negotiated this process.

Key points

- Researchers must collect information from chosen samples.
- The researcher selects a sample from the target population.
- Sampling bias can occur if one element of the target population is over- or under-represented.
- The two strategies used to select a sample are probability and non-probability sampling.
- There are no hard and fast rules about the size of sample needed to support research, though the use of statistical tests in quantitative studies may dictate sample size.

FURTHER READING

Burns, N. and Grove, S. (1993) *The Practice of Nursing Research: Conduct, Critique and Utilization*, 2nd edn. Philadelphia: W. B. Saunders Co.

Floyd, J. (1993) 'Systematic sampling: theory and clinical methods', *Nursing Research* 42(5), 290–3.

Kidder, L. and Judd, C. (1987) *Research Methods in Social Relations*, 5th edn. New York: CBS Publishing.

LoBiondo-Wood, G. and Haber, J. (eds) (1994) *Nursing Research: Methods, Critical Appraisal and Utilization*, 2nd edn, ch. 4. St Louis: Mosby.

Polit, D. and Hungler, B. (1993) *Essentials of Nursing Research: Methods, Appraisal and Utilization*, 3rd edn. Philadelphia: J. B. Lippincott Co.

CHAPTER 8
Understanding data collection techniques

Learning outcomes

On completion of this chapter the reader should be able to
- appreciate the need for reliable and valid data collection methods in nursing research.
- identify the main data collection techniques used in nursing research.
- understand the need to choose data collection techniques appropriate to the research approach and design.
- evaluate the advantages and disadvantages of different measuring instruments.

Key terms

documentary evidence
interview
Likert scale
non-participant observer
observation
observation schedule
participant observer
physiological measures

psychological measures
questionnaire
rating scale
reliability
secondary data collection
validity
visual analogue scale

INTRODUCTION

Research information can be collected in many ways. The researcher's choice of data collection instrument is influenced by the research approach (qualitative or quantitative) and the research questions to be addressed. The researcher must be confident that the instrument or instruments used will collect information relevant to the research question and support the research approach taken.

The researcher is also concerned about the reliability and validity of the data collection method used. Both reliability and validity are important as they afford credibility to the data collection tool and subsequent research findings (Thorndike *et al.*, 1991; cited in Behi and Nolan, 1995a). Polit and Hungler (1993) suggest a valid and reliable instrument will measure what it is expected to measure, and be consistent or dependable in measuring what it is designed to measure. A valid instrument will therefore measure what it is supposed to measure, and a reliable instrument will always measure what it is supposed to measure. For example, the mercury thermometer is seen as a valid and reliable way of measuring temperature. Unless broken, it will measure a patient's temperature when the principles of correct temperature taking are followed, and will measure every patient's temperature in the same way.

It should be remembered that there is always room for error in measurement. For example, if the principles of correct temperature taking are not followed the thermometer may record an abnormally high or low temperature that would not reflect the patient's true temperature. Data collection is therefore open to some inconsistency. Any inconsistency should be acknowledged by the researcher and may lead to the adoption of research practices which will enhance reliability, such as using several data collection methods. If a data collection instrument is not a valid measure and is not recording what it is expected to, then the researcher must look to alternative measuring tools.

The most commonly used data collection instruments will be discussed in this chapter. These include physiological and psychological measures, measurement scales, questionnaires, interviews, observations and documentary sources. The chapter will not discuss the ways in which any information collected through measurement could be analysed, as this is fully considered in Chapter 9.

PHYSIOLOGICAL AND PSYCHOLOGICAL MEASURES

Both physiological and psychological measures are important to nursing practice. Both measures are used on a day-to-day basis to record patient information. Many of these measures provide valuable information for the health care team, and as valid and reliable measuring tools have been used by researchers. There are a variety of measuring instruments available to the researcher, including electronic measures.

The range of valid and reliable physiological measures available is too vast to list. Examples include the sphygmomanometer and electronic dinamap that record blood pressure, mercury, digital and tympanic thermometers that record temperature, clinitests that indicate urine composition, biochemical tests that measure blood composition, and so the range goes on.

Many of these measures have been employed in the collection of research information. For example, Erickson and Yount (1991) compared tympanic and oral temperatures in surgical patients. The research necessitated physiological measurement of temperature and used an infra-red thermometer to record tympanic temperature, with oral temperature being recorded with a thermistor thermometer. Both instruments provided valid and reliable ways of recording oral and tympanic temperature in surgical patients.

There are many psychological measures available to the researcher. For example, the State Trait Anxiety Inventory measures anxiety that increases as a result of threat (state anxiety), and anxiety that is an inherent part of the person's personality (trait anxiety). The measure offers a useful way of recording anxiety level and has been used by many researchers. Leske (1993) used the inventory to record anxiety levels in family members of elective surgical patients. Ferrell-Torry and Glick (1993) used the Spielberger State Anxiety Inventory to measure the effect of using therapeutic massage as a nursing intervention to modify anxiety in patients with cancer. Both Leske (1993) and Ferrell-Torry and Glick (1993) combined psychological with physiological measures, recording the heart rate and blood pressure of the sample.

The researcher needs to select the most appropriate physiological and psychological instruments to use in the research, which should be both valid and reliable measures. In preparation for data collection, the functioning and availability of equipment will need to be considered. Training in data collection methods, including use of equipment, would also need to be complete before data collection can commence.

MEASUREMENT SCALES

Polit and Hungler (1993) suggest a scale is a device which allows the assignment of numerical scores to a continuum measuring attributes, such as the scale that measures weight, the scale that measures shoe size or the scale that records height. Many scales are used generally in society. Within nursing, scales are used to measure specific phenomena and are important to daily nursing practice. Such scales measure pain response, nutritional status and risk of pressure-sore development.

There are a number of valid and reliable scales available for use in nursing research (Oppenheim, 1992; Bowling, 1995), many of which are used in nursing practice. Oppenheim (1992) suggests the researcher may be able to select existing scales that would achieve the desired research outcome, provided copyright is sought. This overcomes validity and reliability issues which can arise when designing a new measuring scale, that would need to be tried and tested before use.

Scales may be the sole data collection instrument used by the researcher, or may be one of many data collection tools employed. Scales may also be included within the design of questionnaires (see later text). Within this chapter, the rating scale, Likert scale and visual analogue scale are considered.

Rating scales are used to attribute a numerical score to an assessment or judgement (Oppenheim, 1992). The respondent is asked a question and then is guided to select from a series of numbered statements the one which reflects their assessment or judgement. The rating scale is used in student nurse assessment of clinical performance. The qualified nurse may be asked, for example, to assess the student's ability to manage the care of a group of patients, and grade the student's performance in relation to a scale of 0 to 5, with 0 being 'cannot perform the skill' and 5 being 'can teach this skill to another'.

The scale may be used in gathering information from patients about the hospital environment, as in Figure 8.1.

Burns and Grove (1993) suggest rating scales are easy to generate, and can offer a useful form of measurement provided the end statements are not so extreme as to affect their selection. The scales are, however, crude measures, and the information generated this way is limited. In the example opposite, the attitude of staff may be rated in relation to one poor experience or one very positive experience; in other words the patient's response can be swayed by one event rather than a general impression.

Please rate from 1 (low) to 10 (high), the following statements
in relation to your hospital stay.

Satisfaction with	Rating
1 Quietness during the day	( )
2 Quietness during the night	( )
3 Choice of food	( )
4 Heating	( )
5 Bathroom facilities	( )
6 Attitude of nursing staff	( )
7 Attitude of medical staff	( )
8 Cleanliness in the ward	( )
9 Comfort of the bed	( )

Figure 8.1 Example of a rating scale

The Likert scale is the most commonly used scale. Named after the
psychologist Rensis Likert (Polit and Hungler, 1993), it is used to
obtain attitude or opinion to preferably ten or more statements. The
scale is a more refined tool that forces the respondent to give opinion
on a series of statements, indicating whether they strongly disagree,
disagree, are neutral or unsure, agree, strongly agree. Usually
the scale includes five values, to which numerical scores can be
ascribed. More commonly, a high score (5) is achieved by agreement
with a positively worded statement and disagreement with a negative
statement (Polit and Hungler, 1993). Figure 8.2 gives an example of
this.

Likert scales were used by McLaughlin (1994) to measure
casualty nurses' attitudes to attempted suicide. Fourteen attitudinal
statements were measured on a Likert scale ranging from 1 to 5
(strongly disagree to strongly agree). The scoring of attitude response
to each statement allowed the researcher to generate statistical
comparisons of attitude with age of respondent and years of service.

In Figure 8.2, the response to statement one receives a score of 5,
as the respondent strongly agrees with a positive statement. If the
respondent had strongly disagreed with the positive statement, a
score of 1 would be allocated. The response to statement two
receives a score of 1, as the respondent has strongly agreed to a
negative statement. To disagree strongly with this statement would
achieve a score of 5.

The scale should be composed of equal numbers of negative and

	Strongly agree	Agree	Neutral	Disagree	Strongly disagree	Score
1 Children behaving badly benefit from individual attention.	✔					5
2 Children behaving badly do not benefit from individual attention.	✔					1

Figure 8.2 An example of a Likert scale used to measure attitudes to discipline in children

positive statements. If the scale included only positive statements, it would be easy for the respondent to select only positive responses, agreeing with all the statements without thought. There is the potential for respondents continually to choose neutral responses and thus give no impression of attitude or opinion. Respondents might also give the response which meets current thinking. Responses to the example in Figure 8.2 might support the no-smacking lobby.

The visual analogue scale is a vertical or horizontal line, 0–100 mm long, with each millimetre representing a numerical score (Polit and Hungler, 1993). The end points of the scale represent extreme values, with the line denoting all values between. The measurement of pain experience can be achieved using a scale with end points representing unbearable pain and no pain, with all other pain experiences being found along the scale. When using the scale, the patient marks along the line the point which they feel represents their current pain response (see Figure 8.3).

In constructing the scale, the values used to identify the end points need consideration, as they must reflect extremes. There may also be potential difficulties in obtaining a true response. In the example opposite, patients may be reluctant to admit to having unbearable pain.

In selecting measurement scales the researcher will need to know which scales are available and be confident that the scales used will be sensitive enough to obtain the responses required. Additionally, the researcher will need to know that the scales are valid and reliable measures.

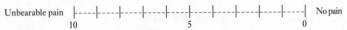

Unbearable pain ┝----┼----┼----┼----┼----┼----┼----┼----┼----┼----┤ No pain
10   5   0

Figure 8.3   An example of a visual analogue scale

QUESTIONNAIRES

The questionnaire is the most frequently used data collection instrument. It is composed of a series of written questions that require written responses. The questionnaire can be used to collect information that is amenable to statistical analysis, and it can therefore be used to collect data in quantitative studies.

The questionnaire offers the researcher flexibility in its delivery, as it can be administered by hand to individuals, to groups of people, or can be posted to reach a large number of people across a wide geographical area. It is often, therefore, the collection instrument chosen for use in surveys. In addition, the questionnaire can be completed anonymously, which can be of value in research studies where honest opinion is sought in a situation of unequal researcher and respondent status. For example, questionnaires can be useful in collecting information from patients, as part of auditing the quality of care being delivered in a particular ward or hospital. The questionnaire proved valuable in overcoming difficulties when student nurses formed a nurse teachers research sample (Moule, 1995).

Whilst reviewing the literature, the researcher may identify a questionnaire that would be an appropriate tool for use in the research study. With the original author's consent, it would be possible to use the same or slightly modified instrument and thus save valuable time in questionnaire generation.

The construction of a new questionnaire requires skill and can be time-consuming. The questionnaire must include questions that will elicit responses needed to address the research question. This process involves using skill and knowledge in questionnaire design. In addition, the researcher would need to establish the validity and reliability of the instrument, using the instrument to collect data, perhaps as part of a pilot study (see Chapter 3).

When formulating a questionnaire, the researcher makes decisions about its structure and layout. The main types of question included are open or closed. Open questions require a response of one or more words or sentences. For example, the question 'In your

Please tick the appropriate response

1   Sex   Male   (   ) 01
               Female   (   ) 02

2   Length of experience in nurse teaching
               1 – 3 years   (   ) 01
               4 – 6 years   (   ) 02
               7 – 10 years   (   ) 03
               11 – 15 years   (   ) 04
               16 – 20 years   (   ) 05
               20+ years   (   ) 06

Figure 8.4   An example of closed questions with coded responses

own words, describe what nursing is' would probably be answered in one or two sentences.

Closed questions are structured to offer the respondent a choice of answers. The scales discussed earlier might be used within this structure. An example of a closed question is seen in Figure 8.4.

Questions should not be leading, such as 'You don't approve of strikes, do you?' nor should they be value laden or ask more than one question at a time. One example of this is the commonly used question 'Do you want tea or coffee?' which is in fact asking two things at once. The organization of questions is also important. Asking sensitive questions at the beginning of the questionnaire can adversely affect response rates. It is usual to establish personal details and ask general questions first, before moving on to more specific and directed questions. The researcher will also need to allow sufficient space for the respondent to give full answers.

Instructions for completion of the questionnaire need to be clear, particularly as the researcher is often not available to clarify any queries. The researcher should include a covering letter of introduction, in which response deadlines may be set and incentives may be offered. It is not uncommon for researchers to offer material reward to those completing a questionnaire.

As part of questionnaire construction the researcher must consider data analysis. Closed questions might be coded, as seen above in Figure 8.4. In question 1, the codes 01 and 02 relate to the sex of the respondents. These codes would be used to prepare the data for analysis. Analysis of open questions would be concerned with identifying specific content, and thus forms part of content analysis, which is discussed as part of data analysis in Chapter 9.

The potential benefits of using a questionnaire to collect research data relate to the effective use of researcher time, reduced costs, access to a world-wide sample, access to a large sample at one time, anonymity and reduced researcher bias. The potential drawbacks can include difficulties in questionnaire construction and exclusion of certain sample groups such as children. The researcher may receive unexpected responses but is unable to pursue these further, as the individual respondents are not identified.

Questionnaires may not be completed by the expected respondent, and additional disadvantages include unsatisfactory completion, rendering the questionnaire useless. Response rates can be poor, with mailed questionnaires often achieving a 25 to 30 per cent response (Burns and Grove, 1993). If a response of less than 50 per cent is achieved, the representativeness of the sample can be called into question (Burns and Grove, 1993). Peters and Lewin (1994) used a postal questionnaire to sample general practitioners. They were able to achieve a response rate of 59.3 per cent, an acceptable and representative sample size.

When response appears low, it is accepted that researchers will follow up the sample with reminders. Response is also aided by providing stamped and addressed reply envelopes, as well as including reply dates as part of an introductory letter. If administered by hand, the researcher might collect the questionnaires or organize a collection point, which will aid response.

INTERVIEWS

Interviews are the second most frequently used data collection technique, and involve the collection of information by verbal communication. Interviews can be conducted on an individual basis, either face to face or over the telephone, or within a group setting. The interview can be used in qualitative research, to collect in-depth information from which a theory can be generated. An interview may also form part of a quantitative design, when a structured interview schedule is used.

The interview schedule is constructed using many of the principles of questionnaire design (see Questionnaires) and would include a list of questions to be posed. The researcher works systematically through the schedule, recording responses. This format can be used in a face-to-face interview or in a telephone interview. Worth and Tierney (1993) used telephone interviews to collect data from elderly people following discharge from hospital. An interview schedule gave structure to the interview and facilitated consistency in data collection.

The approach to interviewing can be less structured, with the researcher identifying one or more key questions that can give some organization to the interview. Individual response to the questions can be explored by the researcher, ultimately allowing the respondent to give direction to the interview. This open design can yield in-depth information about people's opinions, attitudes and feelings, and can be used in individual or group interviews.

The focus group is composed of four to twelve members of differing opinion, who meet to discuss research issues (Morgan, 1988; cited in Reiskin, 1992). The group discussion lasts from one to three hours and is based on outline questions generated through literature review. The facilitator poses the questions or statements, which attempt to answer a research question, and records the group discussion (Reiskin, 1992). The focus group can provide a useful forum for discussing a range of topics, offering the researcher rich data from which further research questions can be generated.

The researcher must decide which interview design will enable the collection of data needed to address the research question. Questions used in an interview must be constructed following the principles of question formation (see Questionnaires). In particular, the content of questions and the organization of questions need consideration.

As interviews necessitate verbal interaction, the researcher needs to consider how to access the sample, making arrangements to conduct interviews at a time convenient to the respondent. The researcher must also consider the duration of the interview, with 30 minutes being a realistic maximum participation time. These points would apply if the interview were conducted over the telephone or face to face. The researcher needs a suitable environment for the interview, with privacy and quietness being important considerations.

The recording of an interview may or may not involve the use of technology. Long-hand recording of interviewee responses is often used and can be preferred by respondents who object to being electronically recorded. However, the researcher might find it useful to record an interview on cassette or video tape. This facilitates analysis of content, as the researcher can listen to the interview several times and, if videoed, may be able to identify non-verbal communication more easily. Audio recordings can be transcribed more readily, which will also aid analysis. The researcher may ask a second person to view or listen to tape, to help with the analysis process. In obtaining a second viewpoint, the researcher may be alerted to new information which had been overlooked, and may be forced to re-examine their perceptions of the interview, thus improving analysis.

Interviewing is a skill that is often presumed to be innate. It is, however, a skill which needs developing, as is depicted by many experienced television interviewers. The researcher is therefore likely to use the pilot study to test the interview schedule or questions, as well as to develop interviewing skills. The interviewer must consider inclinations used in delivering questions as the interviewee might identify these as cues to the sort of response that is wanted. The interviewer has the potential to bias the results in many ways, through non-verbal and verbal cues and by the nature of the relationship with the respondent. A researcher in a perceived position of power may not receive true responses and a researcher seen to be of lower status than the respondent may be dealt with in a dismissive way by the interviewee.

Guaranteed anonymity might overcome some of the difficulties encountered when trying to gain truthful information from respondents. There are potential problems when using vulnerable groups, such as hospitalized patients, as the research sample. The researcher will need to be confident that the patients are enabled to divulge their true feelings and opinions, and acknowledge that the results may be affected by the patients' dependency and vulnerability.

Interviews provide a flexible data collection tool, which can allow the researcher to explore pertinent issues raised during the course of the interview. The interview can provide detailed information, and may also be useful in collecting data from groups unable to respond to a questionnaire, such as children.

The organization of interviews requires thought. Interviews are also more time-consuming, with each interview taking about 45 minutes, 30 minutes of which is spent collecting data. The quality of the information collected may be affected by interviewer bias and the researcher–respondent relationship.

OBSERVATIONS

Nurses are constantly observing patients, using perception and interpretation of what is seen to guide the delivery of nursing care.

Observational studies collect information from observing behaviours or events. Information collected in this way is rarely numerical, but is a record of the researcher's interpretation of events, and is therefore a method employed in qualitative research. It can be particularly valuable in identifying 'hidden' information, of which respondents may be unaware. For example, Littlewood and Saeidi (1994) observed meal times on a psychiatric ward, to see if they could be transformed into a therapeutic experience. They observed patients' food choices, the environment, general atmosphere and interactions between patients and staff. It is unlikely that the patients and staff would have analysed their own behaviour at meal times, so they could not have responded to questions related to this. However, through observation of meal time behaviour, the researchers were able to generate the information required. This example highlights the value of observing events. Observational studies can record the complexity of nursing, which may not easily be measured using any self-reporting methods, such as interviews and questionnaires.

When using an observational approach, the researcher will need to consider the role to be adopted. It is possible for the researcher to be a participant observer or a non-participant observer. The participant observer is part of the situation under observation. If observing activity on a ward, the researcher may assume a nursing role within the ward team. The researcher would therefore be required to fulfil a nursing role as well as a researcher role, which may pose difficulties. There are also issues surrounding the implementation of the participant role. The participant observer may be known to the other members of the nursing team and assume an overt researcher role. Alternatively, the researcher identity may be hidden, with the researcher assuming a covert role. The ethical implications of assuming a covert role tend to limit its use in research.

The non-participant observer would be identified as a researcher, perhaps sitting on the ward observing the delivery of nursing practice. The researcher need not therefore be a nurse, but would need some insight and knowledge of nursing to interpret observations made. The researcher assuming a non-participant role may use more structured data collection tools, such as an observation schedule. The schedule would be predetermined, allowing recording of events under observation in a structured way. For example, the schedule might record verbal interactions with a group of patients on the ward. This would necessitate the recording of the person with whom the interactions are made, and the time taken to complete conversation. The researcher would use codes to identify all possible

Time/Patients	Tony	Alan	Perry	James	Kenneth
0900 hours	A, C	M	D	/	K
0905	/	M	N	I	K
0910	/	M	N	/	K
0915	H, G, F, E	M	C, D	/	K
0920	D, C	H, G, F, E	/	/	K
0925	D, C	/	H, G, F, E	/	O

Key

A	=	health care assistant	I	=	domestic
B	=	auxiliary	J	=	ward clerk
C	=	student nurse	K	=	relatives
D	=	staff nurse	L	=	other patients
E	=	sister/charge nurse	M	=	dietician
F	=	houseman	N	=	physiotherapist
G	=	registrar	O	=	occupational therapist
H	=	consultant	P	=	social worker
			Q	=	other

Figure 8.5 An example of an observation schedule used to record verbal interaction with patients

personnel involved to facilitate easy recording. The end result might appear as in Figure 8.5.

To achieve consistency in measurement, there needs to be parity in the recording and interpretation of information. This can be achieved using recording techniques and through training the observer. In some instances it may be useful to have more than one observer, to overcome difficulties with observer reliability and bias. For example, Rumsey *et al.* (1982) used two observers to record the social distancing used by the public in reaction to a person with facial disfigurement. The researcher's perceptions and interpretations of observations made were tested and found to be reliable.

Recording information gained through observation can pose difficulty for the researcher. A non-participant observer might use an observation schedule, as discussed earlier, or a one-way mirror, or may even record events on video for later analysis. The participant observer needs either to memorize events or find some way of recording field notes.

Access to the sample can also be more problematic. The researcher must organize access to the environment and needs to consider time-management, as it is possible that observations may take from days to weeks or months. There are many issues surrounding the potential affects observational studies may have on the sample, as such studies are more invasive and obtrusive.

Observations can be problematic to the sample, requiring changes to accommodate either researcher or data collection instruments. The constant presence of researchers or data collection instruments may also affect the quality of observation. The 'Hawthorne effect' is a documented account of the effects researcher presence can have on the research outcomes. Researchers considering how to increase productivity at an electrical plant made recommendations based on the increase in productivity seen during their research, which manipulated heating, light and rest time. These recommendations were adopted by the managers, who then saw production fall (Polit and Hungler, 1993). Researcher presence had led to a temporary increase in production. The researcher can therefore introduce bias to the observations by affecting the events observed.

Recording issues relate to the observer role adopted. The non-participant observer may use an observation schedule and find concentration on events easier than the participant observer. There may, however, be ethical dilemmas for the researcher to cope with. For example, if a nurse researcher is recording events in a ward area when a cardiac arrest occurs, there may be a personal dilemma between continuing the observer role and the need to react as a nurse to the situation.

The participant observer may have difficulties recording information, though the information gained may be more insightful. As well as the potential ethical difficulties with assuming a covert role, additional problems may arise if the researcher becomes subsumed into the culture, which would affect objective interpretation of the situation.

Observational studies can provide an in-depth understanding of events, particularly if the researcher has experienced the subject of research. Often observation may be the only technique available to collect information needed. However, observational methods rely on the researcher's perceptions and interpretations of events and can therefore be open to individual bias. There are also organizational issues to consider, including access, recording, role adoption and management of time. Observations can offer the researcher information which might not be obtained using self-reporting techniques; this is particularly evident when considering behaviour and events.

DOCUMENTARY EVIDENCE

Existing documents are a source of research information that forms part of secondary data collection techniques. Researchers are able to access and interpret many health care documents, such as nursing care plans, medical notes, patients' diaries and letters. This facilitates analysis of existing material which has been collected for a purpose other than research, which is identified as secondary data.

Documentary sources have been used in many research studies. Walsh (1990) analysed patients' Accident and Emergency Department admission notes, to explain factors affecting attendance at the department. Reed (1992) examined nursing care plans to analyse the way in which nursing assessment is conducted.

The increased recording of documentary information in health care is likely to provide greater impetus for its use in research. Reed (1992) suggests secondary data sources are likely to gain popularity in the research field, as data recording improves. Polit and Hungler (1993) feel that the reduced costs and time involved in using documentary sources will also be factors affecting their future use.

Other considerations relate to researcher bias, which may be reduced if the researcher was not involved in the initial recording of information. This could be beneficial to the researcher, but may also lead to difficulties if the records are rendered useless because of initial recording problems. For example, the records may be incomplete, inaccurate, or lack data needed for research analysis. When analysing secondary data the researcher must establish the existence and authenticity of records relevant to the research, prior to undertaking the study. Access to relevant records must be negotiated, and sampling issues considered, to overcome sampling bias (see Chapter 7).

Consideration must be given to the analysis of information, collected within one context, but to be used by the researcher in another context, to address a research question. It is possible that analysis by the researcher will ignore the context in which the data were originally collected, and inappropriate judgements may be made. Jacobson *et al.* (1993) suggest that the secondary analyst can misinterpret findings and draw invalid conclusions.

The increased need to record information in health care offers the researcher a wealth of information for consideration. The potential gains from such analysis have been recognized by many researchers and are likely to be considered by many more in the future, despite the potential difficulties which arise from using and analysing secondary data.

Key points

- Research information can be collected in many ways.
- The research approach taken will influence the choice of data collection instruments.
- Reliability and validity are important qualities of any data collection instrument.
- Methods of analysis will need consideration prior to data collection.

FURTHER READING

Bowling, A. (1995) *Measuring Disease: A Review of Disease.* Buckingham: Open University Press.

Burgess, R. (1984) *In the Field: An Introduction to Field Research.* London: Routledge.

Burns, N. and Grove, S. (1993) *The Practice of Nursing Research: Conduct, Critique and Utilization*, 2nd edn, ch. 14. Philadelphia: W. B. Saunders and Co.

McDowell, I. and Newell, L. (1987) *Measuring Health: A Guide to Rating Scales and Questionnaires.* Oxford: Oxford University Press.

Oppenheim, A. (1992) *Questionnaire Design, Interviewing and Attitude Measurement*, 2nd edn. London: Pinter Publishers.

Polit, D. and Hungler, B. (1993) *The Essentials of Nursing Research: Methods, Appraisal and Utilization*, 3rd edn, ch. 8. Philadelphia: J. B. Lippincott Co.

CHAPTER 9
Making sense of data analysis

Learning outcomes

On completion of this chapter the reader should be able to
- understand the difference between descriptive and inferential statistics.
- identify the significance of quantitative results in relation to stages in the research process.
- appreciate the steps required to complete qualitative data analysis.

Key terms

constant comparison
grounded theory
levels of measurement
measures of central tendency

non-parametric
normal distribution
parametric
standard deviation

INTRODUCTION

Many nurses find reading the results and analysis section of a research article difficult to understand. This chapter is aimed at demystifying some of the terminology used in those sections and helping nurses read and interpret the findings of published research.

The type of data analysis the researcher can apply to the data varies according to the approach taken and nature of data collected. Quantitative data analysis will be discussed in the first part of the chapter and emphasis placed on the interpretation of results. In the discussion of qualitative data analysis, the core methods used by researchers from the various qualitative approaches will be identified and examples from current nursing research used to illustrate points made.

DATA ANALYSIS USED IN QUANTITATIVE RESEARCH STUDIES

Descriptive statistics

When a researcher plans their research design they must have some idea of the type of data analysis that will match their approach to the study and the data collecting methods employed. In the first part of the data analysis section of a research article, the researcher usually makes an attempt to describe their results and put them in the context of all the responses obtained.

When asked to describe the age of a group of people, one way it could be done is to give an 'average' age of the group. This is something used in many contexts of everyday life. Averages of different kinds are used in research articles to describe a set of responses. The type of average used depends on the type of data with which the researcher is working.

Below are two questions from a questionnaire which asked student nurses how they had travelled to college that morning and also the distance they had travelled.

(1) Please tick the box which identifies how you travelled to college this morning.

Car	❑	Bus	❑	Motorcycle	❑
Train	❑	Bicycle	❑	Walk	❑
Other	❑				

(2) Please identify to the nearest half mile the distance you travelled to college this morning.

These two questions will produce quite different types of results and because of that will need different kinds of averages. In question 1 the researcher will need to add up all the respondents who ticked each of the boxes and could end up with a list such as this:

Car	64	Bus	11	Motorcycle	5
Train	0	Bicycle	7	Walk	8
Other	0				

To tell us something about the way this group of students travelled to college the researcher will have to identify the means of transport used by most students. In this case, that will be car with 64 – the winner by a long way. In statistical terms data of this type are called nominal as they are collected in named categories and the researcher counts the frequency found in each category. The category that occurs most frequently is called the mode. If two categories have the same frequency the data are called bi-modal; for more than two categories, the term multi-modal is used.

In question 2 the respondents are asked to measure the distance they travelled to college. This is potentially an accurate measurement in which the scale used (miles) is recognized internationally. If one student travelled two miles it would be acknowledged that a student who travelled four miles had travelled twice as far. To tell us about the distances travelled to college by the students the researcher could calculate the average as used in everyday life. That is, add all the distances and divide that sum by the number of students. In statistical terms this type of data is called ratio and the average referred to as the mean.

In between these two categories of data are two more. Ordinal data are measurements which can be put into a rank order but are not measured on an accurate scale. This means that the researcher could put the data in order from lowest to highest or smallest to largest but that is all. A good example of this type of data is the scale used in the assessment of a patient's risk of developing pressure sores. If a group of patients is assessed, the nurse can see who is least at risk and who is potentially most at risk. The score on a visual analogue scale (see Chapter 8) used to measure a patient's pain is also an example of ordinal data. If one patient marked six on such a scale it cannot be said that they had exactly twice the pain of a patient who marked three. However, it might be gauged that they were in more pain at the time.

Because of the inaccuracy of the measurement, a mean should not be used as an average in this type of measurement. Instead, to obtain a way of describing ordinal data, all the measurements are put into a rank order, from lowest to highest or smallest to largest, and the middle measurement of the rank is identified as the median. So, to describe the pressure sore risk factors of a group of patients the

Table 9.1 Summary of levels of measurement and measures of central tendency (MCT)

Data	Characteristics	MCT
Nominal	frequency of categories	mode
Ordinal	no scale but can be ranked	median
Interval	measured on a scale but no zero	mean
Ratio	most accurate, measured on scale with absolute zero	mean

nurse would put the risk assessment scores of each patient in a rank order, from lowest to highest, and find the score exactly in the centre. This would give some indication of the pressure sore risk factor held by a group of patients.

The final category of data that may be used is interval data. These are similar to ratio data but a scale is used in which there is no absolute zero and therefore no fixed point. The example usually given in statistical texts is that of the Fahrenheit scale for measuring temperature. However, as these data are measured on a recognized scale, the mean is the form of average.

These different types of data are called *levels of measurement* and are regarded in a hierarchical order. Statisticians refer to the averages which have been described as *measures of central tendency*. A summary of the levels of measurement and measures of central tendency is seen in Table 9.1.

When using interval or ratio data, researchers can go further in their ability to describe the data recorded from their sample. They can show if their sample had very similar scores or if their scores covered a wide range. To do this the data must be put in a format where not only is the mean identified but also the number of respondents who achieved each score is also identified. Statisticians have found that, if they take any measurement from a random sample of subjects, there will always be a few at the extremes of a measurement scale but most will be clustered around the mean. This is most easily shown in a diagram. Figure 9.1 shows a normal distribution curve, that is, a pattern of measurements shaped like a bell, in which the horizontal axis is the scale of measurements and the vertical axis is the frequency of each of the measurements.

This bell shape can vary between being short and fat, and tall and thin (see Figure 9.2).

The shape of the bell can tell us quite a lot about a set of results

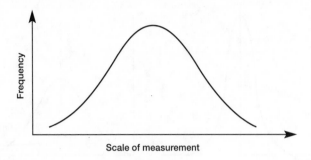

Figure 9.1 Normal distribution curve

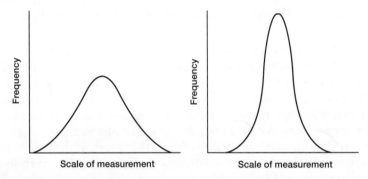

Figure 9.2 Example of different shaped distribution curves

and therefore about a sample. To illustrate this, look at Figure 9.3.

The bell on the left shows the range of ages of patients admitted to a rehabilitation ward the first year after it had opened. It can be seen that ages range from 58 years (the youngest) to 104 years (the oldest) and that the mean age was 81 years.

The bell on the right shows the range of ages of patients admitted to the same ward five years later. The range of ages remains much the same and so does the mean, and yet the shape of the bell is very different. The tall thin bell on the left shows that the ages of a majority of patients were very close to the mean, with very few at the extremes of the age span. However, the bell on the right shows that there were many more patients at the extremes, with far fewer patients clustered around the mean age of 81 years. When comparing these two distribution curves the researcher might begin to think of reasons why these results have been gained and the effect of these changes on the workload of the staff. Reasons for the change might

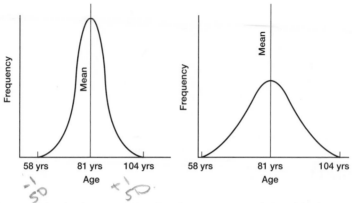

Figure 9.3 Patient age distribution on a care of the elderly ward

include different admissions policy or the opening of other care of the elderly wards in the hospital. The effect on the staff might include the need for a flexible approach to the use of bank staff when there is a higher number of patients aged between 81 and 104 years.

When reading research articles the mean of a set of results might be given along with another figure called the standard deviation (SD). The standard deviation refers to the spread of the results away from the mean. In other words, it is a numerical value given to the shape of the bell curve referred to above. The value of the standard deviation is determined by calculating the difference between each of the scores and the mean, and then finding an average difference.

As standard deviation is calculated on the more rigorous measurements of interval and ratio data, various assumptions can be made from the use of a standard deviation and the bell-shaped curve. Figure 9.4 shows a normal distribution curve with the standard deviation marked in. On each side of the mean there is one standard deviation marked: on the left it is minus one standard deviation and on the right, plus one standard deviation. This allows the researcher to predict, from the sample, the number of the population who will 'fall between' −1 and +1 and −2 and +2 standard deviation.

Sometimes the standard deviation is used to see if two groups are comparable and can be used in further statistical testing. It must be remembered that the standard deviation is always read in conjunction with the mean.

It can be seen from Figure 9.4 that 68 per cent of all cases will fall between −1 and +1, and 95 per cent of the population between −2 and +2 standard deviation. This quite difficult notion can be

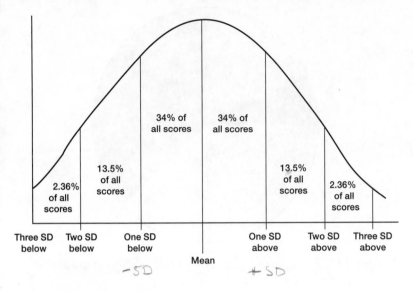

Figure 9.4   Standard deviation

	Pre test	Post test
Mean	5.7	14.8
Standard deviation	2.1	2.6

In the pre test, with a standard deviation of 2.1 and a mean of 5.7, it can be suggested that 68 per cent of the sample had scores between 3.6 (5.7 – 2.1) and 7.8 (5.7 + 2.1).

In the post test, with a standard deviation of 2.6 and a mean of 14.8, it can be suggested that 68 per cent of the sample had scores between 12.2 (14.8 – 2.6) and 17.4 (14.8 + 2.6).

This is dependent on the spread of the scores having a normal distribution.

Figure 9.5   Example of standard deviation (Moule and Knight, 1994)

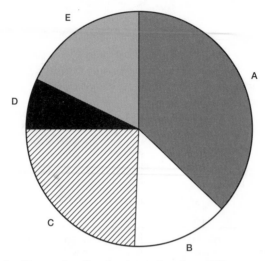

Figure 9.6 Example of a pie chart showing different grades of staff in a medical directorate

explained in the results of a study by Moule and Knight (1994) which examined changes in knowledge and skill of Diploma students (Project 2000) following a basic life support teaching programme (see Figure 9.5).

Another way researchers describe their results is with the aid of pictorial representation. Pie charts such as Figure 9.6 are used in nominal data to show the proportion of each category to the whole set of results.

Each slice of the pie represents one category. Sometimes the sections are simply drawn but other times researchers will actually pull a slice of the pie out to make a particular point. A pie chart is an effective yet simple pictorial representation of a set of results.

Another common representation used to describe a set of results is a bar chart. Bar charts are often used to compare differences between groups or changes in groups (see Figure 9.7).

When looking at both pie and bar charts extremes of measurement should be noted and the questioning process of why these results have occurred should be starting.

Having described a set of results many researchers want then to attempt to give them some meaning. When reading a research article this part of the data analysis usually follows the descriptive statistics and the researcher uses inferential statistics or statistics which infer some meaning.

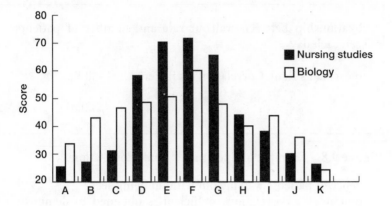

Figure 9.7 Example of a bar chart showing different test results in a group of student nurses.

Inferential statistics

In quantitative studies the researcher frequently looks for a relationship between two or more variables, or a difference between two or more groups. The statistical tests which are used should reflect this.

Tests of a relationship (in statistical terms referred to as a correlation) are chosen according to the level of measurement of the data. The two most common correlation tests are Spearman's Rank Correlation, used for ordinal data, and Pearson Product Moment, used on interval or ratio data. The symbols used to denote these two tests are R_s for Spearman's and r for Pearson. Regardless of the actual test used, a coefficient or figure will be calculated which shows if there is a relationship between the variable, and, if so, how strong that relationship is. A positive correlation indicates that as the measurement of one variable has increased so has the measurement on the other variable. A correlation coefficient between +0.6 and +0.9 shows a strong positive relationship. The closer the figure is to +1 the stronger the relationship. Similarly a correlation coefficient between –0.6 and –0.9 shows a strongly negative relationship. This indicates that as one measurement has increased the other has decreased. A correlation coefficient close to 0 suggests that there is either a very loose relationship or no relationship between the variables. Figure 9.8 shows the results of a study by Walsh (1990) in which he found a positive correlation between the number of patients seen in the Accident and Emergency Department and the

> Relationship between walkout rate and number of patients seen each day
>
> Spearman's Rank Correlation coefficient   = 0.92
>
> $p<0.01$

Figure 9.8   Example of Spearman's Rank Correlation

incidence of patients walking out without being seen.

Sometimes a correlation coefficient is obtained to demonstrate reliability between two researchers who are working together. For example, in a field study by Rumsey *et al.* (1982) in which observers had to stand on one side of a road and calculate the distance individuals stood from a facially disfigured person, a coefficient was calculated to ensure two observers were making similar measurements. With a coefficient of 0.8 the researchers were able to base their results on the measurements of one observer.

There are many different statistical tests of difference used by nursing researchers in their attempt to demonstrate significant findings in their results. As in the measurement of central tendency and the correlation tests, the choice of tests that can be used depends on the level of measurement of the data. Tests which can be used on nominal and ordinal data are referred to as non-parametric and are less powerful than those used on interval and ratio data, which are called parametric tests. To be used, parametric tests also need data which have a normal distribution with samples with similarly shaped bell curves. The most common statistical test used on nominal data is chi-square (χ^2). Non-parametric tests which can be used on ordinal data and look at the difference in the ranking of a data set include the Mann Whitney U test and the Wilcoxon test. Parametric tests which are frequently seen in nursing research literature include the t-test and ANOVA.

To be able to interpret quantitative nursing research it is not necessary to have an in-depth knowledge of these tests, although it is necessary to understand why the tests are performed and how the results can be interpreted. All the tests (both parametric and non-parametric) produce a number – an index – which until recently the researcher would have looked up in a table. When using a computer statistical package such as SPSSX, Easistat or Minitab, the computer 'looks up' the result and prints it out. The result which often concerns nurses reading this type of result looks as follows:

$$p<0.05, p<0.01, p<0.001$$

In this case the p stands for probability and it gives the researcher an insight into how significant their results are and what the probability is that the results occurred by chance. Users of research also need to know how powerful research results are; they are rarely interested in results which could have happened by chance or were a one-off. The three values listed above are sometimes referred to as critical values as they are the levels of significance most frequently quoted in nursing research.

- $p<0.05$ This is the least powerful result usually accepted as significant in nursing research. It means five times out of a hundred these results could have occurred by chance.
- $p<0.01$ This is a more acceptable level and refers to a one in a hundred likelihood of occurring by chance.
- $p<0.001$ This is a highly significant result and the odds of these results occurring by chance have dropped to one in a thousand.

When the result is followed by *ns* it means that the result is *non-significant*. The use of these results is illustrated by a small study by Moule and Knight (1994) who examined the effect of basic life-support teaching sessions using newly designed teaching packs on the basic life-support knowledge of Diploma (Project 2000) students. The data are interval and the t-test was used to examine the difference in the pre- and post-test scores. The computer generated the following highly significant result: $t = 16.109$, $p<0.001$. Thus the null hypothesis that there would be no difference in the pre- and post-test scores could be rejected and the researchers conclude that the teaching session using the new packs made a significant difference to the knowledge level of the students.

Similarly in a study by Wilkinson (1994) on stress among nurses in an oncology unit, the stress levels of staff nurses were compared with the stress felt by other similarly aged working females. Although the comparison between the two groups was non-significant (*ns*), when the researcher looked at the nurses who suffered most stress, significantly high numbers of staff with A levels ($p<0.05$) and who never went to church ($p<0.01$) were found. A further point refers to the phrase 'two tailed test' which is occasionally seen in the description of the statistical test used. It refers to the version of the test used for a null hypothesis.

The more nursing research is read, including these quite difficult statistical results, the more familiar the terminology will become and in time less frightening. This part of the chapter has attempted to introduce some of the issues in quantitative data analysis in a user-friendly way to help nurses of all levels begin to feel a little more confident in reading statistical results.

DATA ANALYSIS USED IN QUALITATIVE NURSING RESEARCH STUDIES

In Chapter 5 it was identified that there are several qualitative approaches to research including phenomenology, ethnography and grounded theory. In Chapter 8 the various research data collecting methods used in these types of research were discussed. However the data were collected or whatever the exact approach used, eventually the researcher will work on the written word. Following data collection the researcher will need to transcribe taped interview recordings and complete observation field notes. The data from open questions on a questionnaire will be ready to work on.

The first task of the researcher is to try and put the data into some order. This is usually done by reading and rereading the data and identifying some preliminary categories which emerge. While selecting these categories there is a sense that the researcher needs both to tell a story and to paint a full picture of the topic under investigation. To do that the researcher must be careful in their choice of categories. Fielding (1993) cites Silvey (1975) when she identifies that all research is about making comparisons of some sort. In order to make those comparisons the data must be organized into some form that allows comparisons to be made. At the preliminary stages of qualitative data analysis a colleague may be asked to read a sample of the data and identify categories. There will then be some comparison of themes and an agreement sought.

Once the categories have been identified the data are scrutinized and a coding scheme devised which incorporates all the categories found in the data. An investigation into why student nurses feel like leaving a Diploma (Project 2000) course during the Common Foundation Programme might generate the following categories.

(1) *Homesickness issues*
  (a) leaving boy/girl friend behind
  (b) never lived away from home before
  (c) no special friendships developed with other student nurses

(2) *Career choice*
  (a) totally wrong career choice
  (b) concern that the Common Foundation Programme is OK but the Branch choice is wrong

(3) *Academic issues*
  (a) only just passing assignments
  (b) the course is too academic
  (c) hate writing assignments
  (d) concern over the academic level required in the Branch

The data would then be read over and over again and coded. Bassett (1994), in his account of a study on nurse teachers' attitudes to research, using a phenomenological approach, describes this reading and rereading as a fascinating experience for him as the teachers appeared to talk freely of their feelings and share their fears of the changes in nurse education as it moves into mainstream higher education. The actual coding might be completed in various ways. Fielding (1993) identifies a scheme for counting the number of times a code occurs in a data set and this allows some numerical analysis of qualitative data. Some researchers mark the transcribed data with the code, while others cut up the pages of transcribed data and put the pieces of data for each code in a separate pile. Agar (1986; cited by Fielding, 1993) originated the analytical method of cutting up the data into strips and literally pasting similarly coded strips onto pieces of card. The use of computer packages for qualitative analysis has eased the situation, although all the data have first to be fed into the computer using a word processor. The computer can then perform basic searches for the coded categories and allows retrieval of the coded segments. For example, in the coded illustration above, all reference to academic work on the Diploma (Project 2000) course could be labelled 'assignments'. The computer could then be asked to search for 'assignments' in a data set and it would retrieve all segments which had been coded in that way. Two of the more common computer packages are ETHNOGRAPH and NUDIST. An in-depth discussion of computer programs for qualitative data analysis is found in Fielding and Lee (1991) and Burnard (1994).

Once the data have been coded the next step is to look for common themes. These might be closely allied to the categories or fall across the categories. Polit and Hungler (1993) suggest that not only should themes be sought but also patterns to the themes. Once these patterns have been identified the researcher might then be able to identify those themes that lie outside the patterns.

Fosbinder (1994), in her study on the way patients see a nurse's competence, used both observations and taped interviews to collect her data. After completing the coding and examining the data, four themes emerged: translating, getting to know you, establishing trust, and going the extra mile. The last theme was identified from patients remarking that some nurses did more than they had to, or that the patients would like to be friends with them after they had left hospital. The analysis was completed using the constant comparative method. In this method, themes are identified early in the examination of the data and then the rest of the data are scrutinized, looking for the themes and constantly comparing the data with the themes. Further examples of constant comparison are found in the discussion of grounded theory.

In his discussion of the analysis of ethnographic data, Fielding (1993) identifies that the researcher must be aware that not all data are equally important and that some confidence must be shown over the selection of the data. Fielding continues to discuss the properties of 'good' qualitative analysis in which there is a reflection of some truth about the phenomenon 'by reference to systematically gathered data' (Fielding, 1993, p. 168). On the other hand, poor analysis does not reflect the phenomena, is descriptive and lacking in any direction.

Unlike quantitative data analysis, in which there is a need to generalize the results from a sample to the research population, qualitative data analysis does not demand generalizabilty. Rather, there is a quest to gain deeper understanding of the phenomenon under scrutiny.

Qualitative researchers attempt to increase the body of knowledge about certain phenomena. In some cases this involves examining data and identifying themes; however, other researchers plan to take their research further and actually develop theories from their data. Grounded theory originated by Glaser and Strauss (1972) is frequently found in nursing research. In these studies, the constant comparison of themes begins soon after the first data are collected. Rather than collect the data in one stage and then move on to the analysis as another stage, grounded theorists examine the early data straight away and devise categories generated by the data to focus the rest of their data collection. As more data are collected it is hoped that more will be revealed about the categories or doubt cast about the wisdom of their selection of categories. This part of the process is called theoretical sampling and continues until the data fail to produce any new categories or information. To help validate the emerging theory the categories may then be applied to a different but similar setting to see if they stand up to testing. This is referred to as comparative sampling and allows the data to be utilized as a body of information constantly being updated and elaborated.

Stern (1980) suggests that the next stage of grounded theory is the identification of a core variable which embodies and identifies the major psychological and social problems in the research. This is illustrated in a study by Hamill (1995) on stress found in Diploma (Project 2000) students in which he used a phenomenological approach and grounded theory for his analysis. Having collected his data using a questionnaire and in-depth interviews, and using a constant comparative method to generate themes, Hamill (1995) identified the dependence/independence continuum as his core variable. He then scrutinized his data to determine the fit of this core variable and found that a majority of the data in which the students identified areas of stress in their lives could be fitted into the dependence/independence continuum. In the college, the students wanted to be treated like adult learners; they were frequently angry that college attendance was compulsory. However, they also experienced difficulty in integrating with the ward team when on their clinical placements. (The sample used by Hamill (1995) was the first Diploma (Project 2000) course cohort and so the ward staff were very unsure of them.) This, Hamill (1995) suggests, fitted into the dependence/independence continuum as the students felt a dependence on the college for support to help them in the strange clinical environment. Grounded theory was utilized by the researcher, as it is used to gain a new insight on a familiar situation in a time of change and the stress among student nurses involved in the move to a Diploma (Project 2000) course appeared to fit into this.

CONTENT ANALYSIS

This system of analysis is almost like a bridge between qualitative and quantitative analysis as there is some measurement involved. It is often used to analyse media coverage of a subject, although it can be used with any form of communication (e.g., health promotion leaflets). When proceeding with this form of analysis the researcher will first decide on the area of interest and then decide on the unit of analysis. This latter could be a word or an inch of newsprint or minutes of television coverage. It could be inches of newsprint devoted to headlines compared to inches of newsprint devoted to editorial. The other measurement employed might be the frequency with which a category appears within each unit of analysis. Some researchers will decide on a list of topics they want to examine and simply sift through the data making a note of whether or not the topic was included. Content analysis could be used to look at the information given to teenagers through the medium of teenage magazines. The researcher would have first decided on a topic in which they were interested, for example advice on contraception. A search of the available magazines would then be commenced, probably looking at a specific range of magazines over a specific length of time. Prior to searching the magazines, the researcher would have decided on the themes they were looking for. These could be:

(a)   the use of condoms
(b)   clinics available for young people for advice
(c)   need for safe sex – not just contraception

or the researcher might be interested in the mode in which any messages were conveyed, e.g.:

(a)   did the characters in the stories discuss sex or contraceptives?
(b)   were there editorials around the issue of contraception?
(c)   the context in which contraception was mentioned in the magazine.

Although not widely used as a means of analysis in nursing research, content analysis is used in health education and promotion research and offers a link between research and a means of communication. It is also used in all forms of historical research when the data are in the form of old documents including letters and reports.

Key points

■ Descriptive statistics describe results.
■ Inferential statistics attempt to infer meaning in results.
■ Different types of written questions produce different levels of measurement.
■ The level of measurement of data dictates the measurement of central tendency and the statistical tests that can be used.
■ Qualitative data analysis uses narrative to identify themes.
■ In grounded theory the data collection and analysis are performed at the same time.

FURTHER READING

Clegg, F. (1982) *Simple Statistics*. Cambridge: Cambridge University Press.
Dale, A., Arber, S. and Procter, M. (1988) *Doing Secondary Data Analysis*. London: Unwin.
de Vaus, D. (1986) *Surveys in Social Research*. London: George Allen & Unwin.
Gilbert, N. (1993) *Researching Social Life*. London: Sage.
Lofland, J. and Lofland, L. (1984) *Analyzing Social Settings*. Belmont, CA: Wadsworth.
Oldham, J. (1993) 'Statistical tests (part 1). Descriptive tests', *Nursing Standard* 7(43), 30–5.

CHAPTER 10
Ethical issues

Learning outcomes

On completion of this chapter the reader should be able to
- understand the nature of 'informed consent' for research subjects.
- discuss the nurse's responsibility to research subjects.
- identify the responsibilities of the nurse as a collector of research data.
- identify the role of Local Research Ethics Committees.
- identify relevant questions that should be considered when reading research reports.

Key terms

anonymity
Code of Professional Conduct
confidentiality

informed consent
Local Research Ethics Committee
vulnerable subjects

INTRODUCTION

More and more nurses are becoming involved in clinical research. A minority are undertaking research projects as part of coursework, and some nurses work as research nurses or are members of a research team. However, there are many more nurses who are marginally involved, perhaps through collecting data from patients and clients, such as urine samples, blood testing or collecting written data for other research workers. These research workers could be doctors, psychologists, health service researchers, sociologists etc., and the nurse may be collecting research data in addition to normal duties. Whether a nurse is the project leader or simply collecting data for someone else, there are responsibilities with regard to the ethics of research on humans. The Royal College of Nursing (RCN) Research Advisory Group (1993) considers that 'each nurse has a responsibility to ensure that research is conducted in an ethically acceptable way' (p. 16) and this doesn't solely mean those nurses who are conducting research themselves. All nurses need to be able to identify and understand any potential ethical problems in a particular study. This is whether they are only superficially involved, or whether they are managing a project themselves. Furthermore, when nurses are critically evaluating research, they need to be able to recognize ethical problems and dilemmas.

INFORMED CONSENT

Informed consent is a concept familiar to many nurses, particularly with reference to treatment and care. The principles of informed consent can also be applied to patients and clients who are potential research subjects. Ayer (1994) considers that there are a number of important considerations when research involves human volunteers, and this includes patients and clients:

- they should know that they are taking part in research
- they should give informed consent to take part in the study
- they should be assured that they can withdraw at any time during the duration of the study.

The Royal College of Nursing Research Advisory Group (1993) recommends that the researcher should also explain how and why participants were selected, and who is undertaking and financing the study. Ayer (1994) submits that certain measures can assist in ensuring voluntary choice and informed consent. This includes providing written information and allowing participants time to consider being involved, before seeking their written consent. Eddie (1994) suggests that informed consent for participation in research also includes an explanation of how long the study is to take, and whether there will be any discomfort for the subjects. In terms of informed consent, Polit and Hungler (1995) summarize this as meaning 'subjects have adequate information regarding the research; are capable of comprehending the information; and have the power of free choice, enabling them to voluntarily consent to, or decline participation in the research' (p. 125).

Polit and Hungler (1995) also suggest that participants should be informed of any conceivable risks or costs, such as psychological or emotional distress resulting from self-disclosure; loss of privacy; loss of time; and any monetary costs that might be associated with participating in the research. Likewise, participants should be informed of any potential benefits, such as material gains, comfort in being able to discuss their situation, escape from normal routine, increased knowledge about their condition, knowledge that they may be helping others, and possibly enhanced self-esteem as a result of receiving special attention. Participants should also be given information about who to contact if they have any questions or complaints relating to the research.

VULNERABLE SUBJECTS

Some people who might be involved in research are considered to be vulnerable subjects. This could be children, people with learning disabilities, and people who have a mental health problem. They are perceived as vulnerable because they may not be capable of giving informed consent to participate in research. Women who are pregnant may also be considered vulnerable because of the high risk of unintended side-effects because of their particular circumstances. In addition to the pregnant woman, there is also a need to safeguard the foetus. Research with vulnerable groups should only be undertaken when there is a high expectation of benefiting the subjects. If a susceptible individual is not capable of giving informed consent, an advocate can consent by proxy on behalf of the individual.

Nurses must be fully aware about the issues surrounding informed consent. If a nurse feels that the patient does not fully understand their role as a research subject, the nurse has a responsibility to make this known to the researcher. Likewise, if a nurse feels that a patient or client wishes to withdraw from a study, or that the research is having an adverse effect on the subjects, she or he has a responsibility to make this known to an appropriate person in authority (RCN, 1993).

THE NURSE AS DATA COLLECTOR

As previously mentioned, some nurses collect data for other research workers in addition to their normal duties. The Research Advisory Group (RCN, 1993) suggests that nurses have an obligation to make it known to an appropriate person in authority if the extra responsibility of data collection becomes detrimental to the normal work of the nurse, or is seen to be having an unfavourable effect on the service. Even something fairly straightforward, like collecting 24-hour urine samples from patients, may become burdensome and demanding of time.

Nurses collecting data for research purposes must be as meticulous, accurate and reliable as they would be in collecting data in their normal work. The Research Advisory Group (RCN, 1993) suggests that there could be a conflict when a nurse takes on a 'dual role' as nurse and researcher. A nurse working in this dual role as practitioner and researcher must ensure that the data collected for research purposes are kept separate from patient information gathered in the normal daily work, unless the subject's consent is obtained. Nurses must also be satisfied that any 'sponsored' research is ethically and scientifically sound and that as individuals they are not associated with any promotion of a particular product (RCN, 1993).

One issue that may create a role conflict when the nurse is a practitioner and researcher is in the area of patient advocacy. The UKCC Code of Professional Conduct (1992) says that the nurse must 'act always in such a manner as to promote and safeguard the interests and well being of patients and clients' (p. 1). If research is undertaken where the intention is to benefit a lot of people and a few patients may suffer as a result of the investigation, there may be conflict with the nurse's role as patient advocate. The RCN (1993) also says that a nurse who is undertaking research must possess the relevant skills and knowledge 'compatible with the demands of the proposed investigation' (p. 11) and acknowledge any limitations of their ability. Nurses must have the necessary research skills if they are working in posts which demand certain expertise. Sometimes the nurse's role is to collect data, and training will be available. However, when the nurse is leading the research, a higher level of knowledge and skills is necessary. This includes literature searching skills (see Chapter 4) to be sure that the knowledge sought is not already available.

Information gathered for research purposes should remain confidential. However, in very exceptional circumstances where this is not possible, participants should be forewarned if confidentiality and anonymity cannot be guaranteed by the researcher. Anonymity can be maintained by not using subjects' names and addresses, and assigning an identity number to participants. Where possible the researcher should not be able to link data with a particular subject. The research subjects should not be discussed beyond the needs of the project, and the data must be kept secure at all times. This is particularly important with data stored on a computer. Access to the data should be restricted to only those people who have a legitimate reason to see them. As Behi and Nolan (1995b) state, 'The collected data need to be received, stored, used and reported in a manner that ensures that no-one but the individual concerned is aware of the source' (p. 713).

RESEARCH ETHICS COMMITTEES

Research that involves patients or clients requires the approval of a Local Research Ethics Committee. A Local Research Ethics Committee will advise its appointing authority, e.g. a Trust, on all matters pertaining to the ethics of research involving human subjects. The membership of a Local Research Ethics Committee will include: medical members, including a general practitioner; non-medical workers, such as psychologists, chaplain, social workers or social scientists; lay people, such as members of the local Community Health Council; and a nurse in clinical practice. There should be no more than twelve Committee members, with both sexes represented. However, the membership will depend to some extent on the authority to which the committee is responsible.

A Local Research Ethics Committee will review proposals for research to be carried out in its own area of authority and will also consider research by the staff of the authority who want to undertake research in other places where there is no Local Research Ethics Committee. A researcher is required to submit a fairly detailed proposal on a standardized application form to the Research Ethics Committee. The form will ask for details, such as the title of the proposed project, the question to be answered, procedures, measurements and data analysis, and the type of subjects, how they will be recruited and how consent will be obtained. The Local Research Ethics Committee will also want to know about the experience of the applicant, the proposed duration of the project and the premises where the research will be conducted. There are specific regulations about drugs that will be a concern to the Committee members, and they will want to know if there are any procedures that may cause discomfort, or be a potential hazard to the subjects. If there is any sponsorship of the research, the Committee will want to know about it. In addition to all of the aforementioned factors, when the Committee considers an application from a researcher it will be judging whether the project is scientifically sound. Local Research Ethics Committees receive guidance from the Department of Health about how they should conduct their business. The Committee must produce reports to the appointing authority on its activity, and these should be made available to the public.

For the nurse who is critically evaluating research, there are a number of questions that can be asked about the ethical acceptability of research. The stages of the research process can be used as a framework to consider questions about ethical issues. Table 10.1 gives some guidelines to assist nurses in critically evaluating the ethical aspects of study. APPENDIX C

Format for Literature Review

Table 10.1 Points to consider when critically evaluating the ethical aspects of research

The purpose of the study	• The knowledge sought should not already be available.
	• The reason for the research should be important.
	• The resources for the study should be adequate.
	• Potential outcomes of the study should be realistic (e.g., if a study is trying out a very expensive treatment, is it likely to be implemented if the outcome is favourable?).
	• The research should not be undertaken solely for the researcher's benefit (e.g. career development).
	• Sponsored research should be carefully considered.
Research problem	• The problem should be researchable and all potential ways of solving the problem should be considered.
	• Research questions and hypotheses should be developed directly from the problem.
	• The investigation of certain problems may not be feasible because it places unethical or unrealistic demands on subjects.
Literature search	• A good range of literature should be thoroughly searched.
	• The review should be balanced and not biased.
	• Conflicting evidence should be clearly presented.
	• Quotes and citations should be within the context of the original study.
	• Limitations of the literature cited should be identified.
	• Copyright regulations must not be broken.

'' margin

- There should be no evidence of plagiarism or mis-quotation.

Sample selection
- The researcher should have made a good attempt at selecting an appropriate sample.
- If a random sample has been selected, this should be genuinely random.
- There should be no coercion in recruiting subjects.
- There should be evidence that the subjects have given informed consent and know that they can withdraw at any time.
- Were the subjects a vulnerable group?
- If patients are involved, the proposed research must have been approved by a Local Research Ethics Committee.

Data collection
- The researcher should have used an appropriate method of data collection related to the research questions.
- The subjects should be protected from physical and psychological harm.
- The method of data collection should not have been selected because it is a preferred or accomplished technique of the researcher.
- How was the issue of 'deception' dealt with in observational studies?
- The method of data collection should not have been chosen with the intention of gaining particular results.
- The data should be gathered by appropriate people.
- In qualitative studies, what was the researcher's role and relationship with the subjects?

Results and analysis of findings
- The results and analysis should not be manipulated in order to favour particular findings.
- All the results should be given, not only the researcher's preferred ones.
- There should be no evidence of lost or destroyed data.
- In qualitative studies, how did the researcher remain true to the data?

Conclusions, recommendations and limitations
- The researcher should base the conclusions and recommendations on the results of the study.
- There should be no intention to mislead or give false conclusions.
- The sample selected should be considered in relation to the recommendations.
- The researcher should acknowledge any limitations in a comprehensive way.
- Limitations of the findings of the study should be identified, as well as limitations of the study design and techniques.

Dissemination	• The researcher should be disseminating the results appropriately and fully.
	• If only sections of the study are disseminated, this should be clearly explained.

General points

- Was there evidence that privacy, dignity, anonymity and confidentiality were maintained throughout the study?
- The researcher should not be attempting to confuse or deceive the reader.
- The reader should acknowledge sources of support and funding.
- The reader should 'feel' that the researcher has integrity and is honest.
- Did the benefits of the study outweigh the potential risks?
- The researcher should have identified ethical issues related to the study.
- The reader should acknowledge their own limitations in critically evaluating research, and gain assistance when necessary.

(Adapted from Hek, Judd and Moule (1996))

Key points

- Nurses must be aware of ethical issues when they are reading research.
- Informed consent is an important consideration in all research involving human subjects.
- Some research subjects, such as children and people with a mental health problem, are considered vulnerable.
- Confidentiality and anonymity should be maintained.
- Local Research Ethics Committees serve the interests of patients with regard to research.
- There are a number of ethical points to consider when reading research.

FURTHER READING

Ayer, S. (1994) 'A proper process of scrutiny', *Professional Nurse* 9(9), 595–9.

Behi, R. and Nolan, M. (1995) 'Ethical issues in research', *British Journal of Nursing* 4(12), 712–16.

Eddie, F. C. T. (1994) 'Moral and ethical dilemmas in relation to research projects', *British Journal of Nursing* 3(4), 182–4.

King's College (1993) *Manual for Research Ethics Committees*. London: King's College.

Polit, D. F. and Hungler, B. P. (1995) *Nursing Research: Principles and Methods*, 5th edn. Philadelphia: J. B. Lippincott Co.

Royal College of Nursing Research Advisory Group (1993) *Ethics Related to Research in Nursing*. Harrow: Scutari Press.

United Kingdom Central Council for Nursing, Midwifery and Health Visiting (1992) *Code of Professional Conduct*, 3rd edn. London: UKCC.

CHAPTER 11
Critical evaluation of nursing research

Learning outcomes

On completion of this chapter the reader should be able to
- appreciate the need to critique research.
- identify the strengths and weaknesses of qualitative and quantitative research.
- critically evaluate a nursing research journal article.

Key terms

critically evaluate   critique

INTRODUCTION

Nurses need to be able to critique research for many different reasons. In Chapter 1 the term 'research literate' was used as a basis for discussion. This discussion centred on the need for nurses to be able to appreciate the skills and knowledge required to understand and use research to provide quality and effective care. One result of having those skills and that knowledge is the ability to evaluate the many research articles in journals. Several years ago the term 'research has shown' was enough to justify almost any nursing care. These days that is not enough: nurses must be able to rationalize their care explicitly and show that the specific research used was worthy of their consideration.

Evaluative and critical skills are used in our everyday life. Every time a decision is made in the supermarket about which brand of toothpaste or shampoo to buy, influences such as marketing, the media, experiences, the family tradition, and cost are exerted. So these skills are not new, but they do need to be developed and applied to the world of nursing research.

Before critiquing research it is important to recognize that critiquing does not necessarily mean being negatively critical. Critiquing is more about looking for strengths and weaknesses in a study in the light of the reader's knowledge and the manner in which the research has been presented. Polit and Hungler (1993) suggest that when identifying both strengths and weaknesses all decisions need to be supported and justified.

Developing critical evaluation skills has become crucial to all nursing students regardless of the course they are following. Many courses ask for a research critique within their assessment scheme to demonstrate critical evaluation skills. Other courses ask for a rationalization or discussion of nursing care, demonstrating the academic skills of critical thinking or critical analysis. Acquiring the skills required to evaluate nursing research critically depends on practice and thoughtful reading of research articles and reports. Appendix 2 (p. 136) contains a critical evaluation checklist of questions to ask when critiquing a research paper. At first this is hard work; the language can appear alien, sometimes the results are written in a format that appears to require high levels of statistical knowledge to interpret, and altogether the nurse is left feeling bewildered.

A worthwhile introduction to reading research and developing critical evaluation skills is to read several research articles, which all address the same (or similar) topic. This topic should be one in which the reader is particularly interested, either for an assignment or because they feature a specific care issue. It is surprising how an interest in a specific subject helps overcome some of the immediate problems of reading research. The other point which must be recognized is that not all parts of the research need to be understood in the first couple of readings. However, gradually, as knowledge is increased, more and more will be understood.

LoBiondo-Wood and Haber (1994) suggest critical evaluation first involves several readings of the same article (accompanied by a research textbook) in which to 'identify concepts, clarify unfamiliar terms, question assumptions and determine supporting evidence'. They also list four stages of understanding through which the reader should pass. These are:

- preliminary
- comprehensive
- analysis
- synthesis

At the first stage, the reader is directed to skim read the abstract and headings, followed by the rest of the article, highlighting or marking any unfamiliar words. To be able comprehensively to understand a research article, LoBiondo-Wood and Haber (1994) suggest that the reader should be able to discuss the article. Reaching these two stages of understanding should allow the reader to break down the study into constituent parts (analysis) and build it together again and evaluate whether it makes a whole picture or if there are identified weaknesses.

SETTING THE RESEARCH SCENE

In the first part of the article the author should identify the purpose of the study and why the research needs to be completed. This might be because a problem was identified in clinical practice or because it was necessary for a course. Whatever the reason, all research should add to a body of knowledge, either by identifying more questions to ask, at one end of the continuum, or by adding substantive findings following large-scale testing of theories, at the other. There needs to be some reassurance from the researcher that the study will fulfil this requirement.

Unless the researcher has identified that they are using grounded theory and are purposely not looking at the related literature until later in the study (there is some debate about this – see Talbot, 1995), the literature review should provide a background to the study. In the literature review there should be a comparing and contrasting of the literature, not simply a description of it. The strengths and weaknesses of previous studies should be identified and the dates of the studies should be noted. Although the literature review should include any authoritative or classic work on the topic, regardless of age, there should be an attempt to embrace the most recent work as well.

Following on from the literature review, the researcher should establish a focus of the study. In a quantitative study this should be a defined focus, often in the form of a hypothesis, but it could also be a question or an aim (see Chapter 6). If there is a hypothesis it should be seen to emerge from the literature and it must be relevant to the topic being studied. The wording of the hypothesis should be clear and at least two variables identified. It should also be clear whether the researcher is looking for a relationship between two or more variables or for differences between groups. When critically evaluating a quantitative report the reader should check to see that, if the researcher has used a null hypothesis, the statistical analysis includes a two tailed test of significance (see Chapter 9). In qualitative studies there should be a focus for the study in the form of aims, objectives or questions. These can be scrutinized for their relevance to the research approach and the literature review.

In both qualitative and quantitative studies the aims, questions or hypotheses should be examined to see if they link the previous work completed in this topic area with the research about to be undertaken. By keeping this as a central focus when critiquing a study, the reader can often discover inconsistencies, either with the literature and the approach or the literature and the design. In order to do this the reader must be familiar with the purpose of research aims, questions or hypotheses.

COLLECTING THE DATA

One of the ways the researcher can demonstrate their creativity is in the design of their study. There should be some indication of how they decided on their eventual research design – the influences and the constraints. The researcher should be able to demonstrate that the chosen design is appropriate to the study. For example, Rumsey et al. (1982) used observations in their study of people's behaviour when confronted with someone with a facial disfigurement. An alternative might have been to interview people and ask them about their behaviour when confronting a facially disfigured person. With a little thought it might be seen that most respondents would talk about how they think they would behave and this might be quite different from how they actually do behave. Therefore, interviewing respondents could be seen as an inappropriate data collection technique in this instance.

The heart of a research critique lies in an evaluation of the way in which data were collected to solve the research problem. In any critical evaluation there should be an exploration of alternative strategies to the one presented. Once the design has been examined and the data collection technique has been evaluated the sample selected needs careful scrutiny. The appropriate size of the sample will differ depending on the research approach used. In qualitative studies a small sample is used to gain in-depth information. Even with a small sample, the selection of individuals for the sample should be justified by the researcher. In some qualitative studies the researcher might focus on particular respondents because of a specific interest. Particularly in a grounded theory approach the researcher will look at the early data received and use them as a guide for the subsequent data collection. This should be explained and rationalized in the study.

When critiquing deductive studies the reader should examine the sample very carefully. The whole thrust of studies which attempt to test a theory using a quantitative data collection technique is the transfer of the results from the sample to the research population. In an attempt to eradicate bias the researcher should strive to use a random sample in which everyone in the target population has an equal chance of being included. As most research studies have constraints on them in terms of cost, a totally randomized sample is rarely seen in nursing research. However, the implications of the sample composition should be included and allowed for in any discussion of the results and their generalization. The sample should also mimic the target population in terms of its constitution. A quick look at a research study to see how the sample and target population match up in their constituent parts will give the reader an insight into the research (see Chapter 7). For example, if the researcher has generalized their results to all Diploma (Project 2000) course students, the question arises as to whether the sample includes students following all four Branches of the course or whether they used their local College of Health for their sample, which doesn't provide the Mental Health Branch. The finer points of sample selection should also be addressed. For example, if a stratified sample was used with insufficient numbers in the smaller strata, it may make a difference to the results. Such a sample of student nurses might reveal a small number of Mental Health, Learning Difficulties and Child Branch students in the sample, with an overwhelming number of Adult Branch students. The researcher would need to explain the implications of the sample used.

In all research, the data collecting method should be described as well as rationalized. An example of the data collecting tool should be included, as this allows an examination of the questionnaire or interview schedule. Any measuring tool should also be included along with a discussion on how it was tested for reliability and how the individuals collecting the data were trained in its use. A demonstration of the deductive researcher's commitment to accurate measurement of the variables will enhance the whole study. At this point in the study there might be a description of the pilot study. This should indicate any changes made to the data collecting tool and identify any problems the researcher found with the research design. It can take some honesty for the researcher to identify such problems. If there are no results of the pilot study given, the reader is left unsure what the researcher found and insecure of the reliability and validity of the data collecting methods used.

When critically evaluating a questionnaire there needs to be an examination of the types of questions used and their relevance to the approach taken. A qualitative approach will demand a majority of open questions which allow the respondent to explain exactly how they feel or think. The closed questions and measuring scales found in quantitative studies should be examined for their ease of use, their clarity and the clarity of the instructions given for their use.

In observational studies there should be some indication of how obvious the observer was, if it was covert or overt observation, and the role the observer played. If it was overt observation, did the researcher include the effect of researcher presence on any results? The researcher should also detail how the field notes were recorded and when full notes were written up. If it was more than 24 hours after the observation their accuracy and completeness must be seriously questioned.

Accounts of the research study should give the reader sufficient detail to allow such a replication. In an attempt to evaluate an investigation the reader should be able to look over the whole of the research design to see if it could be used as a basis for another study, using the same approach, data collecting methods, measuring tools and methods of analysis.

RESULTS AND DATA ANALYSIS

Possibly the one section that nurses feel least able to critique is the result and analysis section of a research study. The first area that needs to be examined is the relevance of the results to the research approach taken. If an inductive approach was taken the results section should demonstrate the emergence of themes from the data. Results should not necessarily offer an explanation but may simply offer the reader an account of the findings. In such research reports the researcher should indicate how the results were authenticated. This might involve triangulation, when two methods could be used to collect the same information, for example in-depth interviews and observations of behaviour. In the search for themes from qualitative data, a colleague might be asked to identify themes from a sample of the responses to see if there is agreement. Whatever form it takes, the researcher should show any steps that have been taken to demonstrate the trustworthiness of the data (Polit and Hungler, 1993).

In research in which the variables were measured, the results section should give the full range of responses. The beginning of the section should also identify the response rate from any questionnaires used. A description of the results might include pictorial representation such as pie or bar charts, tables or graphs. These can aid enormously in helping the reader get an overview of the results. All sections of any diagrams should be examined for accurate labelling, otherwise the reader is left trying to guess what is being referred to. The diagrams should also be clear and able to 'stand alone' – if they require text to explain them they are usually inadequate.

In deductive analysis the researcher should justify the use of specific statistical tests. The reader should be able to see a clear link between the research approach, the level of measurement gained from the data collection tool, and the statistical tests used. The level of significance produced by the statistical testing should also be examined to ensure it is above the 5 per cent level ($p<0.05$). In nursing research, if there is a greater than 5 per cent probability that the results occurred by chance, they are usually deemed non-significant (see Chapter 9).

CONCLUSIONS AND DISCUSSION OF RESULTS

One of the dangers in any research report is that the researcher will attribute more meaning to the results than the analysis will support. In moving from the data analysis section to the interpretation and conclusions the reader should be able to follow a logical progression. Any generalization made by the researcher should be examined in the light of the results section and of the selection of the sample used. One of the most frequent problems with nursing research is seen when a small sample is used in a deductive study with quantitative techniques of data collection and analysis. Following statistical testing with significant results the researcher 'forgets' the size and constitution of the sample. The researcher should not be criticized for using a small sample but could be criticized for generalizing the results from the sample to the target population without acknowledging the limitations of the study. The results should be examined in the light of any hypothesis which should be accepted or rejected.

It is important to remember that nothing in research is ever proved (see Chapter 6) as there is always an element of chance in the results or error in the data collection methods.

Nursing research should always address the implications for practice that the findings have. At the end of the day nursing research is about adding to a body of knowledge which includes both the practical aspects and the organization of nursing. The message throughout this book is that critical evaluation is the key to the utilization of research by nurses. There should always be an identifiable link between the research and the world of nursing.

> **Key points**
>
> - It is essential that all nurses develop critical evaluation skills.
> - In order to understand research articles it is necessary to read them several times.
> - The inexperienced reader may find the use of a critical evaluation checklist useful (as found in Appendix 2).

FURTHER READING

Avis, M. (1994a) 'Reading research critically: I. An introduction to appraisal designs and objectives', *Journal of Clinical Nursing* 3(4), 227–34.
Avis, M. (1994b) 'Reading research critically: II. An introduction to appraisal: assessing the evidence', *Journal of Clinical Nursing* 3(5), 271–7.
Burns, N. and Grove, S. K. (1993) *The Practice of Nursing Research: Conduct, Critique and Utilization*, 2nd edn. Philadelphia: W. B. Saunders Co.
LoBiondo-Wood, G. and Haber, J. (eds) (1994) *Nursing Research: Methods, Critical Appraisal and Utilization*, 3rd edn. St Louis: The C. V. Mosby Co.

CHAPTER 12
Disseminating nursing research and the way forward

Learning outcomes

On completion of this chapter the reader should be able to
- recognize and appreciate the need for dissemination of research in nursing and the health services.
- identify mechanisms for dissemination of research in nursing and the health services.
- appreciate some of the problems of research utilization in nursing and the health services.
- acknowledge the responsibilities of the nurse with regard to dissemination and implementation of research.
- identify education and training opportunities.

Key terms

Centre for Reviews and Dissemination
Cochrane Collaboration
research dissemination

'Research for Health'
research implementation
Taskforce Strategy
A Vision for the Future

INTRODUCTION

In this book we have constantly highlighted the need for nurses to recognize the importance of using research in their daily practice. We have used the now common term 'research literacy' to describe the skills that nurses need to enable them to gain access to relevant literature, and to be able to read and critically evaluate research. By developing these skills, nurses will be able to assess the appropriateness of using research based evidence in their daily practice in order to provide the highest standards of patient care possible. In addition, they will be able to contribute to the identification of research problems and priorities that may need to be investigated.

Many researchers have explored the reasons why research findings do not get translated into practice (e.g., MacGuire, 1990; Bassett, 1992; Closs and Cheater, 1994), and (although perhaps outdated) Hunt (1981) is one of the most frequently cited studies. Hunt (1981, p. 192) identified five main reasons why nurses do not use research findings:

1 they do not know about them
2 they do not understand them
3 they do not believe them
4 they do not know how to apply them
5 they are not allowed to use them.

The nurse who is becoming research literate is already tackling points 2 and 3 by gaining a greater understanding of the process of research and exploring the ways that nursing has developed its knowledge. To a certain extent, point 1 is being addressed through nurses recognizing the need to find out about research themselves by developing skills to search and retrieve literature (see Chapter 4). This final chapter also confronts point 1 by exploring ways in which research findings are disseminated by researchers, and, although noting some of the problems of inappropriate and ineffective dissemination, will consider the ways that dissemination can be improved. This chapter also considers the complex issue of the research/practice gap and problems of research application and utilization, focusing on the ways in which research findings can be implemented in nursing practice.

DISSEMINATION OF RESEARCH

Researchers have a responsibility to ensure that their research findings are appropriately disseminated to relevant people, either verbally or in writing. These people may include academic colleagues, fellow researchers, educationalists and practitioners, or members of professions associated to nursing such as medicine, health promotion officers, dieticians, pharmacists, physiotherapists etc. The most important people, however, are those who are able to act on the research in some way, and these are likely to be practitioners, managers and educationalists. Researchers are often criticized because they tend to publish in journals not routinely read by nurses in practice. An example might be publishing an article in the *Journal of Advanced Nursing* rather than the *Nursing Times* or the *Journal of Community Nursing* which are more commonly read by practitioners. Nursing journals are a very important source of research, and researchers need to carefully consider where to publish if they want their research to be read by nurses who are in a position to do something about the findings. Researchers also have a responsibility to clearly identify the implications of their research for nursing care and nursing practice. This is becoming a requirement for publishing in many of the nursing journals today.

The Department of Health's Research and Development Strategy 'Research for Health' (Department of Health, 1993c) re-examines the purpose and organization of health research. One of the objectives of the strategy is to 'ensure that the benefits of research are systematically and effectively translated into practice' (p. 2), and this is identified through the provision of a structure for disseminating research and development to users. Information systems are being set up to provide research results in an accessible form by documenting on-going research and facilitating the transfer of research findings into practice. The Projects Registers System (PRS) has been established to record all projects supported by the National Health Service. Although still in its infancy, the intention is that the register will eventually link up with other databases related to health (see Appendix 1).

The Cochrane Collaboration based in Oxford was set up in 1992, and has been established to provide information about existing research evidence. It assists specialists to prepare, maintain and disseminate systematic up-to-date reviews of randomized controlled trials of health care. The Collaboration already produces the Cochrane Pregnancy and Childbirth Database (see Appendix 1). The Centre for Reviews and Dissemination (CRD) at York has also been established as a result of the National Research and Development Strategy (Department of Health, 1993c). The Centre complements the work of the Cochrane Collaboration by commissioning systematic reviews beyond the sphere of controlled trials, particularly in the areas of effectiveness and cost-effectiveness of health care interventions.

There are other initiatives that support the dissemination aspects of the National Research and Development Strategy (Department of

Health, 1993c). The National Health Service Management Executive sponsors the production of *Effective Health Care* bulletins. These provide research based information that is relevant to clinical and managerial decision-makers. Some Regional Research and Development Directorates also disseminate 'research based evidence' through newsletters. An example is *Bandolier* which is produced by the Anglia and Oxford Region, and *Evidence-Based Purchasing* which is produced by South and West Region.

The South and West Research and Development Directorate also produces briefing papers which provide summaries of existing research evidence on a particular topic. Some examples are the use of steroids before pre-term delivery, the use of thrombolysis in acute myocardial infarction, and the use of *helicobacter pylori* eradication therapy in the treatment of duodenal ulceration. These papers are of some interest to nurses.

The *Report of the Taskforce on the Strategy for Research in Nursing, Midwifery and Health Visiting* (Department of Health, 1993b) welcomes the attention given by the National Research and Development Strategy (Department of Health, 1993c) to the importance of dissemination of information generated from research and development. The Taskforce recommends that nursing, midwifery and health visiting projects should be incorporated into the overall developments of National Research and Development Strategy such as the Projects Register System and the work of the Centre for Reviews and Dissemination and the Cochrane Centre. The Taskforce also recognizes that the links between research and practice cannot be a 'top-down' communication of research findings to practitioners. They want better and closer relationships between researchers and practitioners and they believe that this could happen through the development of centres of excellence for the development of research led practice.

A Vision for the Future (Department of Health, 1993a) also acknowledges the importance of disseminating research findings. In particular, it recommends the establishment of 'networks to disseminate practice informed by research findings' (p. 14). This could mean, for example, the establishment of research interest groups or journal clubs, which are becoming increasingly popular. McCloughlin *et al.* (1993) describe how they formed a research interest group in Northern Ireland. The aim of the group was to 'enable nurses to work towards research-based clinical practice' (p. 52), and their first task was to attempt to demystify research. The group viewed the critical assessment of research as one of the most important skills to enable them to differentiate between 'good' and 'bad' research. The Group comprised nominated nurses who represented each clinical area, and they gathered research articles of direct relevance to their area of practice. These nurses would then, with the help of the overall group, critically assess the research for its relevance and appropriateness and then relay the information back to their own clinical areas. The Research Interest Group was fortunate as they had the support of management, who provided secretarial and administrative help. Aspery (1993) also describes how she set up a journal club for neonatal nurses. As with McCloughlin *et al.* (1993), the club encouraged the critical evaluation of research in relation to clinical practice. These examples demonstrate ways in which targets from strategies such as *A Vision for the Future* (Department of Health, 1993a) can be put into practice through the insight of a number of individuals who try to bridge the gap between research and practice, with the aim of improving patient care.

McIntosh (1995) asserts that clinical nurses need time and motivation to read, in addition to critical appraisal skills, if they are going to be able to identify research of value and importance. There is a responsibility for managers to recognize this and provide nurses with the necessary time and support. Target nine of *A Vision for the Future* places responsibility on the 'providers' by recommending that they should be able to demonstrate areas where 'clinical practice has changed as a result of research findings' (p. 14). For this target to be realized, there must be support and encouragement for nurses not only to recognize research of relevance, but also to be able to utilize and implement research into their daily practice.

UTILIZATION AND IMPLEMENTATION OF RESEARCH

The problem of utilization and dissemination of research is not confined to nursing (Hunt, 1987; Hardey, 1994). In nursing, the successful utilization of research findings is complex (Closs and Cheater, 1994) and there are a number of barriers to implementation. Despite a certain amount of attention (e.g. Hunt, 1981), it is not helpful for nurses to be 'blamed' for not implementing research findings and evidence in their daily practice. MacGuire (1990) suggests that the problem of utilization of research findings has been oversimplified in terms of why nurses in clinical practice do not examine their practice. Research findings may question the personal beliefs and values of individual nurses, who may be caught up in traditional and ritualistic practice (see Chapter 2) where they have found it difficult to challenge the *status quo*. Becoming research aware may assist nurses to acquire a greater understanding of how knowledge is developed within the profession, and consider a need to change current practice. Individual nurses may be enthusiastic and committed. However, they may not be allowed to implement research findings because of cost or staffing implications, or because they challenge established nursing practice. Hunt (1981) makes an important point which is as relevant today as in the 1970s and 1980s: 'Those with the authority to effect change do not want to, and those who want to innovate do not have the requisite authority' (p. 194).

MacGuire (1990) considers a number of different levels at which the implementation of research needs to be thought about, and examines the uptake of research findings as a consideration within the overall management of change. MacGuire (1990) is eager not to blame any one group, for example practitioners, researchers, educationalists; and suggests that the integration of research and practice has to be confronted at all levels within an organization. There have been some attempts made to overcome the problem of the gap between research and practice. Hardey (1994) discusses the creation of new nursing roles such as 'nurse researcher', 'research nurse', 'clinical nurse researcher'. These types of appointment have become common in the United States of America and Canada and are becoming a more familiar sight in the United Kingdom, although there is scope for further development. One of the aims of these posts is to combine research and practice with a nurse who has clinical obligations in addition to research or educational responsibilities. Another 'joint' role described by Wilson-Barnett *et al.* (1990) is that of 'researcher as teacher'. She cites two case studies of the 'nurse researcher–teacher' role where the researcher was directly able to benefit patients, relatives and nurses. The combined research/practice/education roles are not without problems, however, and the difficulties are often the result of conflicting responsibilities and accountability. The establishment of such joint positions needs careful consideration and planning, as well as constant monitoring, if the individuals are to succeed in implementing research and making a change to nursing practice.

Closs and Cheater (1994) suggest a number of actions that can be taken to promote the utilization of research, including joint researcher/practitioner appointments and collaborative projects. They also suggest that research teaching should be incorporated into pre- and post-registration nursing curricula, and that the time and skills necessary to use research resources should be facilitated. The English National Board's response to the Strategy for Research (English National Board, 1994) also acknowledged the importance of education by stating: 'The Board will strive to develop the research appreciation and research skills of the professions ensuring that the content of the education programmes it approves is based wherever possible on research findings *and* education programmes contain research appreciation' (p. 2).

Hunt (1987), Webb (1990) and Titchen and Binnie (1994) propose approaches such as 'Action Research' as a means of challenging some of the problems of research utilization and getting research into practice. From the investigator's perspective, Closs and Cheater (1994) suggest that researchers should find 'ways of presenting their findings in a clear, accessible and easily understood form for clinical nurses to use' (p. 771). They conclude by suggesting that an underlying principle is for nurses to develop a positive research culture with interest and support for the promotion of research utilization. English (1994) also says that all nurses should accept some responsibility for increased research commitment.

EDUCATION AND TRAINING

The Taskforce Strategy (Department of Health, 1993b) recognizes that research skills and experience in nursing need to be 'far more widespread than at present' (p. 12). As previously noted, there is no expectation that all nurses should be *doing* research, but rather that all nurses should be research literate, with a minority of nurses making a career in research. For those nurses wishing to pursue a research career, the strategy calls for expanded access to research training. This includes post-graduate taught research courses, research training positions, funding for research studentships and post-doctoral research fellowships. There is also recognition that research supervision and secondment opportunities should be further developed.

For the majority of nurses, becoming research aware is the main concern. As a result of the recent changes in nurse education leading to courses at Diploma level (Project 2000), newly qualified nurses should be more research aware. However, for established practitioners who missed out in their initial training, there is a need for continuing education. The Taskforce Strategy (Department of Health, 1993b) uses the term 'catch up' courses; it suggests that these should enable qualified practitioners and managers to 'deepen their understanding of research processes and the utilisation of research findings' (p. 13). One such course is the ENB 870, 'An Introduction to the Understanding and Application of Research', which concentrates on enabling nurses to become research aware. There are also other short courses on research awareness that are designed for nurses in clinical practice. The opportunities for nurses to become research literate are expanding, and nurses should seek support to enable them to gain knowledge and skills that they can apply to their own area of practice.

The *Report of the Taskforce on the Strategy for Research in Nursing, Midwifery and Health Visiting* (Department of Health, 1993b) has been good news for nursing in many ways. It has given the nursing profession recognition with regard to research and has identified a number of worthwhile recommendations to give direction. Nurses have a responsibility to find out about research in their own area of clinical practice and should not expect to be passive recipients of research. All nurses need to develop and use skills to retrieve and assess research critically. This requires an understanding of the sources of research literature, and how to search and obtain research relevant to practice. Such skills will enable nurses to evaluate research findings critically and assess the appropriateness of using research based evidence in their daily practice. With adequate education, support and encouragement, the complex issues of research utilization and implementation will be confronted and reconciled. Nurses will be confident that they are providing the highest standards of care possible for their patients and clients.

Key points

- There are complex reasons why research findings do not get translated into practice.
- The National Research and Development Strategy has implemented a number of information systems for disseminating research and development.
- Nurses need to consider ways of implementing research based evidence into clinical practice.
- There are a number of education and training opportunities for both nurses in clinical practice and nurses who may wish to pursue a career in nursing research.

FURTHER READING

Bassett, C. (1992) 'The integration of research in the clinical setting: obstacles and solutions. A review of the literature', *Nursing Practice* 6(1), 4–8.

Closs, J. S. and Cheater, F. (1994) 'Utilization of nursing research: culture, interest and support', *Journal of Advanced Nursing* 19(4), 762–73.

English, I. (1994) 'Nursing as a research-based profession: 22 years after Briggs', *British Journal of Nursing* 3(8), 402–6.

MacGuire, J. M. (1990) 'Putting nursing research findings into practice: research utilization as an aspect of the management of change', *Journal of Advanced Nursing* 15(5), 614–20.

McIntosh, J. (1995) 'Barriers to research implementation', *Nurse Researcher* 2(4), 83–91.

Wilson-Barnett, J., Corner, J. and De Carle, B. (1990) 'Integrating nursing research and practice – the role of the researcher as teacher', *Journal of Advanced Nursing* 15(5), 621–5.

APPENDIX 1

Sources of nursing research literature

- Nursing and professional journals which contain comprehensive research articles.
  E.g. *Journal of Advanced Nursing, Nurse Researcher, Nursing Research, Journal of Clinical Nursing, International Journal of Nursing Studies, Intensive and Critical Care Nursing.*
- Indexes and abstracts that list articles and reports under subject headings.
  E.g. CINAHL, *The Nurses and Midwives Index* (NMI), *The International Nursing Index, Health Service Abstracts, Nursing Research Abstracts.*
- Current Awareness bibliographies and bulletins that list recent papers under subject headings.
  E.g. *Palliative Care Index, Ethnic Minorities Health, British Institute of Learning Disabilities* (bild).
- Published research reports from various origins.
  E.g. Government departments, English National Board, university departments, research units, specialist units, written reports for the funders of the research, charities and voluntary organizations.
- Conference papers that have been produced as a result of a national or international conference.
- Specialist books sometimes report research studies on a specific subject topic. Usually the books are edited and each chapter has a different author who has undertaken research in the subject area.
  E.g. *Recent Advances in Nursing: Issues in Women's Health* (Hardy and Randell, 1989).
- Theses and dissertations which are produced as the result of research undertaken for a degree. These are usually available at

the university where the degree was undertaken and can be borrowed for a short while, either fully bound or as a microfiche. The Royal College of Nursing has a collection of nursing dissertations – the Steinberg Collection – and the British Library also keeps a list of theses.

Useful information resources for nurses

- The English National Board for Nursing, Midwifery and Health Visiting has the Health Care Database available on-line on ENB Campus through Campus 2000. It includes details of books, reports, journal articles, research projects, open-learning material, computer packages and audio-visual material. You can also request a free search by telephone, letter, fax or electronic mail.
- The Royal College of Nursing Library has information on books, journal articles, reports, theses and videos. An information service is currently free to members.
- The Health Visitors Association has a collection of material of interest to health visitors, school nurses and other community nurses. The service is currently free to members.
- The King's Fund Centre Library has a database on health and social care management. The library is open to visitors, and literature searches of the database are currently free.
- The Nuffield Institute for Health Information Resource Centre keeps a database called Health Management Information Service (HELMIS).
- The UK Cochrane Centre in Oxford produces the Cochrane Pregnancy and Childbirth Database and the Cochrane Database of Systematic Reviews.
- The Centre for Reviews and Dissemination (CRD) at York keeps a database of good quality research reviews of the effectiveness and cost-effectiveness of health care interventions, and the management and organization of health services. It also keeps a database of published economic evaluations of health care interventions.

APPENDIX 2

Critical evaluation checklist

Questions to ask when critiquing a research paper:
- Why has the researcher chosen to study this particular phenomenon/topic/subject?
- What is the original research question/problem?
- Does the literature review include literature from the last five years?
- Is the literature review organized in a systematic way (i.e., in themes or subjects)?
- Is the hypothesis/aim/question consistent with the research approach?
- Is there an account of how the data were collected?
- Is the data collecting/measurement tool included?
- Is the sample randomized and representative? Does it matter?
- Are the results clearly identified?
- If the study is deductive, does the analysis refer to the hypothesis/aim/question?
- If the study is inductive, has the researcher taken steps to authenticate the data?
- Can the results and analysis be linked back to the original research question?
- Have the findings been related to nursing?
- Is the author of the research credible as a nurse and a researcher?
- What steps were taken to ensure all stages of the research were ethically sound?

GLOSSARY OF TERMS

abstract	a brief summary of a piece of research which identifies the main stages of the research process
action research	an approach to research which attempts to bring about change as a result of reflection on practice. The researcher works alongside practitioners in order to effect change
anonymity	ensuring non-identification of research subjects or organizations, so that they cannot be linked with the data being collected
bias	an unintentional influence or effect which may occur at any stage of the research process and which distorts the findings (e.g. sample bias, interview bias)
case study	in-depth study of an individual or organization
CINAHL	*Cumulative Index to Nursing and Allied Health Literature.* A database found in printed or computerized format
common sense	knowledge that is commonly accepted
concept	an abstract idea which may be informed by previous experience or knowledge
confidentiality	ensuring data are used only for the purpose for which they are gathered and that information gathered cannot be linked to an individual
content analysis	the processing and interpretation of non-numerical data, e.g. examining text in great depth for recurring words or themes
control group	subjects that do not receive an intervention or treatment in an experiment
correlation coefficient	a figure calculated to demonstrate the size and direction of relationship between two variables

critical evaluation	identifying the strengths and weaknesses of research, by considering each stage of the research process in some detail
critique	a critical evaluation of a particular study including its limitations and importance
data analysis	the processing, summarizing and interpretation of raw data into meaningful information
deductive	a process by which general principles or theories are applied to a particular situation
Delphi technique	a technique for gathering views or opinions or judgements from a group of experts
descriptive statistics	the use of various statistical techniques to describe numerical data, e.g. mean, standard deviation, variance
dissemination	ensuring the results of research are communicated to a wide audience
ethnography	a research approach which usually involves the researcher studying individuals or groups in their natural setting
experiment	a scientific research design which tests a hypothesis and whereby subjects are randomly allocated to different groups (see control group; experimental group)
experimental group	subjects that receive an intervention or treatment in an experiment
external validity	the extent to which findings can be generalized to other populations or situations
feminist research	a particular research approach which seeks to empower women
gatekeeper	a term often used to describe a person or persons who are attempting to safeguard the interests of others
generalizability	the degree to which the researcher can transfer research findings from the studied sample to a target population
grounded theory	a qualitative approach to research which uses the process of inductive reasoning to develop theory from specific observations
Hawthorne effect	an effect which occurs as a result of subjects knowing they are involved in a study
hypothesis	a measurable statement which sets out the expected

relationship between two or more variables

implementation	the development of techniques to promote and support the utilization of research
inductive	a process by which principles or theories are developed from a particular situation or observation
inferential statistics	the use of various statistical techniques to either infer meaning from the sample to the target population or demonstrate the strength of a relationship between variables
informed consent	obtaining verbal or written permission from an individual to voluntarily take part in a study
interviews	a data collection technique that involves gathering information through verbal communication, often using a schedule, e.g. telephone interviewing, one-to-one interviews, group interview
intuition	insight that is developed through experience
Likert scale	a refined measurement scale that requires the respondent to give opinion on a series of statements
literature review	a section of a report, or a whole report where previous research or literature or a specific subject has been examined or reviewed
literature search	systematic and thorough exploration of literature (e.g. journal articles, books, reports) on a specific subject
longitudinal study	a study by which the same subjects are studied at different points over a period of time
mean	the arithmetic average of a set of scores
median	the mid point in a set of ranked scores
medical model	approach to health care which is derived from medical knowledge and practice
mode	the most frequently occurring characteristic in a data set. Where *two* characteristics occur most frequently, the term bi-modal is used
non-parametric tests	a group of statistical tests used to identify differences or relationships between variables. Suitable for ordinal or nominal data
non-participant observation	a technique for gathering observational data where the researcher is detached from the situation being studied

non–probability sample	the researcher is unable to state the statistical likelihood of a member of the target population appearing in the sample. The selection of the samples was by non-random techniques
null hypothesis	a statement which predicts that there will be no relationship between identified variables. Sometimes known as a statistical hypothesis
observation	a data collection technique that involves gathering information through visual means, e.g. watching, sometimes using a schedule to record the observations
parametric tests	a group of sensitive and powerful statistical tests used to identify differences or relationships between variables and which are applied to interval or ratio levels of measurement
participant observation	a technique for gathering observational data where the researcher is part of the situation being studied
phenomenon	an event studied by the researcher
phenomenology	a research approach which examines the lived experiences of individuals from their own perceptions
pilot study	a small preliminary study that allows the researcher to test the research methodology, e.g. data collection techniques
probability	the likelihood of research findings occurring by chance, which may be identified by a p value
probability sample	a sample selected randomly, allowing the researcher to state the statistical likelihood of a member of the target population appearing in the sample
qualitative data analysis	processing and interpretation of non-numerical data, e.g. words and text
qualitative data collection	gathering non-numerical data such as words and text, through various techniques, e.g. interviews and observations
quantitative data analysis	processing and interpretation of numerical data
quantitative data collection	gathering primarily numerical data through various techniques, e.g. structured questionnaires, measuring scales, physiological measurements
quasi-experiment	an experiment-like study which is not able to conform to all the requirements of an experiment

questionnaire	a data collection instrument composed of written questions that require written responses
randomized controlled trial	an experiment conducted in a clinical environment
raw data	information that has been systematically collected by the researcher, prior to processing
reflective practice	systematically looking back and learning from past practice and experience
reliability	the extent to which an instrument or technique shows consistency of measurement
replication	repeating another researcher's study using the same techniques as in the original research
representative sample	the degree to which a sample has the characteristics of the research population
Research Ethics Committee	a group of people who meet regularly with a common aim of judging the appropriateness and scientific merit of proposed research. Usually linked to an organization, e.g. District Health Authority, Health Care Trust, university
research question	a specific question that the researcher is seeking the answer to through investigation
retrospective study	examining data that have been collected in the past. It is often used for the purpose of establishing a relationship between variables
rituals	routine and unquestioned actions
sample	a portion or part of a population, from which data can be collected
sampling	the techniques used to select a portion or part of a population
sampling bias	over- or under-representation of characteristics of the target population found in the sample
sampling error	problems resulting from the sampling technique, which lead to the generation of a biased sample
sampling frame	a record of all members of the population from which a sample can be selected
scientific knowledge	knowledge verified by systematic and rigorous enquiry
secondary data	the extraction and use of data that have been previously collected for another purpose, e.g. hospital admission rates

sources of knowledge	different types of knowledge that can be used as a basis for decision-making
standard deviation	a figure calculated to identify the spread of the data set around the mean
statistical significance	the extent to which results are 'real' rather than due to chance
target population	the entire membership of the group in which the researcher is interested and from which data can be collected
theory	a structured collection of ideas or concepts which seeks to explain or describe phenomena
tradition	continued use of past actions or customs which may or may not have lost their meaning
trial and error	trying different ways of solving a problem until a solution is found
triangulation	the use of two or more research approaches, data collection methods or analysis techniques in the same study
utilization	the use and application of research findings to inform decision making and practice
validity	the extent to which an instrument or technique measures what it is intended to measure
variables	a characteristic that varies between individuals and can be measured or manipulated in the research, e.g. age, pain, height, gender

REFERENCES

Abbott, P. (1993) 'Why do we need to review literature?' *Nurse Researcher* 1(1), 14–22.

Agan, D. (1987) 'Intuitive knowledge as a dimension of nursing', *Advanced Nursing Science* 10(1), 63–70.

Aggleton, P. and Chalmers, H. (1986) 'Nursing research, nursing theory and the nursing process', *Journal of Advanced Nursing* 11(2), 197–202.

Argyris, L. and Schon, D. (1974) *Theory in Practice*. San Francisco: Jossey Bass.

Aspery, C. (1993) 'How to set up a journal club', *British Journal of Midwifery* 1(1), 17–20.

Ayer, S. (1994) 'A proper process of scrutiny', *Professional Nurse* 9(9), 595–9.

Bassett, C. (1992) 'The integration of research in the clinical setting: obstacles and solutions. A review of the literature', *Nursing Practice* 6(1), 4–8.

Bassett, C. (1994) 'Nurse teachers' attitudes to research: a phenomenological study', *Journal of Advanced Nursing* 19(3), 585–92.

Behi, R. and Nolan, M. (1995a) 'Reliability: consistency and accuracy in measurement', *British Journal of Nursing* 4(8), 472–5.

Behi, R. and Nolan, M. (1995b) 'Ethical issues in research', *British Journal of Nursing* 4(12), 712–16.

Benner, P. (1984) *From Novice to Expert: Excellence and Power in Clinical Nursing Practice*. California: Addison-Wesley.

Berg, B. L. (1989) *Qualitative Research Methods for the Social Sciences*. London: Allyn and Bacon.

Bowling, A. (1995) *Measuring Disease: A Review of Disease*. Buckingham: Open University Press.

Brink, P. J. and Wood, M. J. (1978) *Basic Steps in Planning Nursing Research: From Question to Proposal*. North Scituate, MA: Duxbury.

Buckeldee, J. and McMahon, R. (eds) (1994) *The Research Experience in Nursing*. London: Chapman & Hall.

Buenting, J. (1992) 'Health life-styles of lesbian and heterosexual women', *Healthcare for Women International* 13(2), 165–71.

Burnard, P. (1989) ' The sixth sense', *Nursing Times* 85(50), 52–3.

Burnard, P. (1993) 'Facilities for searching the literature and storing references', *Nurse Researcher* 1(1), 56–63.

Burnard, P. (1994) 'Using a database program to handle qualitative data', *Nurse Education Today* 14(3), 228–31.

Burnard, P. and Morrison, P. (1990) *Nursing Research in Action: Developing Basic Skills.* London: Macmillan.

Burns, N. and Grove, S. (1993) *The Practice of Nursing Research: Conduct, Critique and Utilization,* 2nd edn. Philadelphia: W. B. Saunders and Co.

Carper, B. (1978) 'Fundamental patterns of knowing in nursing', *Advances in Nursing Science* 1(1), 13–23.

Castledine, G. (1994) 'Finding funds for nursing research', *British Journal of Nursing* 3(22), 1197.

Clark, E. (1987) *Sources of Nursing Knowledge,* Research Awareness Series, Module 2. London: Distance Learning Centre.

Closs, S. J. and Cheater, F. M. (1994) 'Utilization of nursing research: culture, interest and support', *Journal of Advanced Nursing* 19(4), 762–73.

Cook, J. A. and Fonow, M. (1986) 'Knowledge and women's interest: issues of epistemology and methodology in feminist sociological research', *Sociological Enquiry,* Winter, 2–29.

Cormack, D. (ed.) (1991) *The Research Process in Nursing,* 2nd edn. London: Blackwell Scientific Publications.

Cuzzell, J. and Stotts, N. (1990) 'Trial and error yields to knowledge', *American Journal of Nursing* 90(10), 53–9.

Department of Health (1993a) *A Vision for the Future.* London: Department of Health.

Department of Health (1993b) *Report of the Taskforce on the Strategy for Research in Nursing, Midwifery and Health Visiting.* London: Department of Health.

Department of Health (1993c) *Research for Health.* London: Department of Health.

Department of Health and Social Security (1972) *Report of the Committee on Nursing.* London: HMSO.

Depoy, E. and Gitlin, L. N. (1994) *Introduction to Research: Multiple Strategies for Health and Human Services.* St Louis: Mosby.

Eddie, F. C. T. (1994) 'Moral and ethical dilemmas in relation to research projects', *British Journal of Nursing* 3(4), 182–4.

Ellis, J. (1995) 'Testing the feasibility of timed district nurses' visits', *Nursing Times* 91(3), 40–1.

English, I. (1994) 'Nursing as a research-based profession: 22 years after Briggs', *British Journal of Nursing* 3(8), 402–6.

English National Board for Nursing, Midwifery and Health Visiting (1993) 'Research components of Certificate/Diploma level programmes', *ENB News* 8(3).

English National Board for Nursing, Midwifery and Health Visiting (1994) *The Board's Response to the Strategy for Research.* London: English National Board for Nursing, Midwifery and Health Visiting.

Erickson, R. and Yount, S. (1991) 'Comparison of tympanic and oral